WOMEN:

THE LAST

CHANCE FOR

AFRICA

Christian Igodo

FOREWORD

By Her Excellency DrJustinaMutale

"Women are the Pillars of Africa and are the ones who will bring Africa's prosperity back..."

- AfrikaKongo Queen

The message in the above quote is reflected in the United Nations Global Goals for Sustainable Development (SDGs), which have at their core gender equality and the empowerment of women as a priority, with gender equality cutting across all the 17 goals of the SDGs. The emphasis on gender equality and the empowerment of women in the SDGs indicates that the world cannot achieve any or all of the Sustainable Development Goals without securing the full and equal rights of women, who form half of the world's population. Indeed, Africa as a Continent cannot achieve prosperity without utilising half its manpower, half its human resource and half its human potential, which is imbedded in the women of the Continent.

African women and their potential contributions to political participation, economic advancements, social progress and environmental protection have over the years been marginalized. In failing to utilise the potential and talents of their female populations, African countries have been under investing in the human capital needed to assure sustainable development for the Continent.

Africa is a growing economy and at the centre of this growing Continent are women ready to make a difference.

Africa is the richest and yet the poorest Continent in the world, feeding the rest f the world with its abundant wealth from minerals, precious stones to other raw materials and natural resources in addition to manpower. Africa has an opportunity to can change for the better by utilising the skills and wisdom of its women to capitalise on the Continents abundant wealth. However, institutional discriminationand other circumstances beyond their control, continue to limit the potential of African women to fully contribute to building the economy of the Continent. The best investment Africa can make is to put capital in the hands of women to work on behalf of its young generation and to make women and young people more creative and more innovative by allowing women to unleash their potential to develop Africa and to maximise the potential of the Continent.

Most of the world's written history has depicted women in African societies as dual minors. And for the most part, the story of African women and girls has been told through the shadow of the father and then that of their husband, but this is not a true reflection of the African society that I know. Long before the rest of the world embarked on moves towards gender equality, most African women already carried leadership roles in their communities. The historical heritage of many African countries is rich with women who protected and fought for the rights of their people. And yet these women continue to be ignored in the history books.

For thousands of years, African women were equal, if not superior, to their men. For thousands of years, many African societies were matriarchal, they were led by strong, powerful, assertive, wise women. And these societies prospered. However, colonisation brought with it the shift from a subsistence economy to a monetary economy based on remunerated employment, and this overturned all the benefits of a matriarchal society and reinforced men's supremacy over women in Africa. This made Africa's women's bargaining power and position weak in respect of access to and control of their resources. It also reduced African women's level of participation in decision-making and the process of development.

I believe the 21st century is a century to reawaken the feminine spirit in Africa and to bring out the feminine wealth to empower humanity in order for the Continent and the rest of the world to secure human prosperity. I believe that the rising of women in Africa would be the awakening of humanity, thereby paving a path to human prosperity.

According to Jim Kim, President of the World Bank, countries around the world and in Africa in particular, pay a big price by failing to realise the potential of women. A recent study of the world Bank report found that women account for only 38% of their country's human capital wealth, versus 62% for men. If this gap were closed in 141 countries according to the study, the world would generate $160 trillion in additional human capita wealth. Mr Kim reiterates that the world bank encourages and supports investment in women's education, workforce, development and entrepreneurship to realize the rising aspirations of developing countries and to build the human capital needed for the economy of the future.

The pursuit of sustainability for Africa therefore, should start with giving women opportunities for the advancement of the Continent. Africa has choices to make and these choices should put women at the centre. This requires transforming policies and a different mindset. Africa needs to break its structural barriers, which are faced by its women and girls including conscious and unconscious bias and institutional discrimination. In order to fully develop the its economy, Africa needs to take its women on board to build the Continent and drive the agenda for the Continent's sustainability, not just because this is the right thing to do, but because it is the smart thing to do. Like the rest of the world, Africa cannot achieve the critical Sustainable Development Goals without securing the full and equal rights of half of the Continent's population. Therefore, the creation of an *African Women's Development Bank* is a critical call to action.

For centuries now, the world economy and that of Africa has been modelled on male perspectives. To date, women in Africa continue to be denied equal opportunity to participate in decisions that affect their lives, whether in the public or private sphere, from the highest levels of government decision-making to households.While Africa has had some of the fastest growing economies in the world in recent years, with some African countries becoming top performers in the world economic league, it has also become common place to find that while there has been accelerated economic growth there has at the same time, been rising levels of unemployment and poverty, coupled with falling levels of education and health care provision.This has largely been attributed to the current economic model, which is largely built on the ambitions and perspectives of men. The male economic model, which puts profit and unnecessary competition as a priority without due consideration to human consequences has failed Africa, because the masculine spirit is only concerned about the self, while the feminine sprit is about building the family, children, community, country, world and planet.

I must commend Christian Igodo on his work in *"Women: The Last Chance for Africa"* which aims to build solidarity among African women, to enable African women to rise to the challenge of liberating Africa from its economic predicament. Christian's work brings to the fore the negative effects on the economy of Africa, resulting from denying women's participation in building the economy of the Continent. *"Women: The Last Chance for Africa"* is a result of pensive research and exposition of economic and development efforts in different countries in Africa, compared with the entrepreneurship of women.

The creation of the *African Women Development Bank* would be a radical development model aimed at reviving Africa's economy and putting money in the hands of those who need it the most. The *African Women Development Bank* would be a great economic and development model for the Continent, which strongly advocates for the empowerment of the African Continent through its women, who are the custodians of power, king makers, nation builders, and pillars of Africa. Women are the last chance for Africa, because women are the ones who will bring back Africa's rightful and God-given prosperity.

Her Excellency Dr JustinaMutale
President, JustinaMutale Foundation
African Woman of the Year (2012)
100 Reputable Africans in the World
Co-author, *"Women on Corporate Boards: An International Perspective"*

DEDICATION

To the departed souls of women and children.

To the great souls that have migrated to the other side of existential reality.

The great African and their children who toil, suffer to remain, grow and blossom and add beauty and rhythm to our collective existence, but are denounced, frustrated and suffocated to stillness and death.

To you, we doff our hat. With due humility, spiritual commitment, zeal, persuasion, tears, anguish and most of all love, we pledge solemnly to carry along the struggle.

To you great mothers that toil day and night to produce enough to take care of the family under terrible conditions, fear, terror, pain, insecurity, torture, rape, maim and death!

To you that love us, to you that is sincere, giving much towards the benefit of all, while mindless, restive, conscience less, retrogressive, repressive, barbaric, greedy, selfish, visionless, mindless, senseless, satanic, war mongers and ridiculous rascals ravage, destroy and loot the gain of your toil and sweat.

To you we say with honour and humility cheer up, the end to this epoch of ruin has come, the locust years are over, a new dawn has come with a new order and a new life, now is the day for change, we cannot defer on convening the conference urgently! **African Women Development Bank Project.**

To you who were not involved in the struggle for power, through war never design, engage, destroy or invent weapons of mass destruction!

To you who do not loot the remaining scarce resources, to you who do not divert funds made for the promotion of our collective welfare into private pockets.

To you we pledge to continue the struggle for equity and accountability without restraint!

To you whom so much, love peace and progress shown by your great radiance of warmth and promise.

Like the morning sun and a blossomed rose on a summer morning giving joy and peace to all.

To you we have resolved to follow, to work for. If need be lay down our life, until the entire resources and buildings of authority and power is under your total control!

To you who love progress, the time has come, the hour has come.

Take charge! And take control!

To you Oh mother we dedicate all.

Table of Content

CHAPTER ONE

INTRODUCTION

"Alternatives must be identified, must be given legitimacy and must set in motion. Political and economic alternatives are the hope of the third world"… Paulo EvaristoArns.

The purpose of producing this literary work: *"The Last Chance for Africa"* is to build solidarity among African women, to enable them rise to the challenge of extricating Africa from the deep mess which irresponsible leadership and visionless governance have put her into in recent times.

The work honestly portrays the irrationality of denying culpability by Africans of the present misery and squalor ravaging the continent by blaming the western world for the problems of the continent.

This work; after honest exposition of the mindless pillaging and destruction of the Africa through endemic corruption, and moral decadence, violence and instability, by its visionless and ridiculous leadership; totally negates all the conventional development models operating in the continent, as they are stagnant and retrogressive, and replaced them with a realistic, pragmatic and result-oriented development model which will place political and economic power on the people; particularly women and not irresponsible rascals and war-mongers.

The bold development initiative for Africa as advocated in this work; The African Women Development Bank on-line, "money must go to those who need it project", is a negation of the age long convention of barbaric and retrogressive government in Africa controlling economic power while the citizenry, particularly women, die in squalor, misery and penury. The Western World represented by its establishments and institutions cannot exonerate themselves from the present economic handicap of Africa owing to its involvement in slavery, colonialism prescription of economic policies of doubtful value such as Structural Adjustment Programme (SAP), which worsened for instance economic crises in Nigeria, aiding and supporting unpopular governments, receiving and safe guarding looted funds by irresponsible African leaders and unfair trade environment promoted by World Trade Organization (WTO) and General Agreement on Tariffs and Trade (GATT). African leaders on the other hand are the worst culprits of the heinous crime committed against the continent.

Africa is grappling with deep economic crises, characterized by poverty, instability, disease, insecurity and social stagnation, while its leaders are engaged in mad and senseless misappropriation of scarce resources.

The last chance for Africa is a results of pensive research and exposition of economic and development efforts in different countries of Africa, compared with the entrepreneurship of women.

In a sense, the agonizing reoccurring experience of and mindless wastage of resources and lack of vision by African leaders with the seeming conspiracy of Western Donor Agencies in sustaining this retrogressive development paradigm in Africa, call for the urgent need for an alternative and realistic approach to solving Africa's problems, hence-*The Last Chance for Africa*. The African Women Development Bank on-line is a radical development model aimed at giving money to those who need it through proper documentation of the practices of the rural women associations and cooperative societies in Africa for onward disbursement of funds to them. It is a new economic and development model for the continent that strongly advocates the empowerment of the African women.

The major preoccupation of African women, are cash crops production and small-scale industrial production, crop processing, food preservation, handicrafts, food processing, catering, trading and small scale industries.

It is the above-named activities that sustain Africa from eminent death caused by deep-rooted corruption and mismanagement of our human and material resources. Yet women are still grossly marginalized, victimized and abused in Africa.

There are yet culturally-induced violence such as female genital mutilation, widowhood practice, rape, killing, and female trafficking.

At the root of all these abuses are economic, political discrimination as well as marginalization, which sustain them all.

The marginalization of women in Africa has cost the continent a great deal in its question to self-sustenance, growth and development.

Cultural and official impediments that stand on the way of women to fully partake in the production of goods and creation of services must be removed while capital and natural resources in the continent must, as a matter of urgency, be managed by women before the little that is left of the African soul is carted away by greedy, irresponsible and short-sighted men in positions of authority in different African countries.

Contemporary development in the global arena has clearly indicated that the rescue and survival of Africa must emanate from within and that segment of Africa that are free from the ethical and physical error sustaining that caused the contemporary anguish and shame in the continent that immensely qualified for this great task.

We cannot continue to go to the western countries cap in hand; rather we should look inwards and work zealously with discipline and organization to salvage ourselves from the present mess.

While working pensively to develop a model that would propel the renaissance of Africa, we should appreciate the approach and method which other continents adopted to propeldeveloping countries adopted to promote their economic development and see its relevance in the African context.

The remarkable development strides that were witnessed in the Asian countries of Japan, China, Malaysia, Taiwan, South Korea, Singapore, Hong-Kong were as a result of empowerment of its citizenry economically through the provision of credit facility. This approach assisted the citizenry tremendously to embark on industrialization which in turn promoted their domestic products, generated growth in national income and finally give them a remarkable development.

In Africa, the large number of our population are engaged in small-scale industrial productions and subsistence agriculture. African women form a major portion of this bloc. They are the segment that, through their activities, are the engine room that propel Africa's economic development. If only this portion of Africans could be empowered economically, there would be an assured remarkable development in the continent. It is these segments who earnestly need financial aid for meaningful engagement in production of goods and services. Their modest engagement in farming, food processing and small-scale industries will make a remarkable difference in Africa's quest for sustainable development.

Modern financial and economic theories tend to neglect the social and cultural realities in different societies, rather they promote cosmopolitan ideologies that have made worse the precarious economic situation of African countries of which women and children are the most affected.

Contemporarily, Africa is faced with the challenge of living with worsening economic situation in an unfair global environment. The major problems facing Africa include stiffening debt profile, unfair global trade environment which promote the advantage and interest of the developed world on the other hand, as well political instability, war and destruction in almost all parts of Africa.

The attendant consequence of this detestable state of affairs is the total impoverishment of the citizenry, particularly women and children. The penury, squalor and poverty which state corruption and human-mismanagement have brought to Africa are lamentable and monumental. It permeates all strata of existence: high mortality rate, malnutrition and impoverishment, unemployment, crime, high rate of preventable diseases and general societal insecurity.

Two major factors are responsible for this unfortunate state of affairs, namely:

1. EXTERNAL INFLUENCE

Under external influence, one considers the negative effects of slave trade on the physical and psychological being of Africans. The over six hundred (600) years of trade interaction between Africa, Western and Arabic world affected the social and economic development of Africa adversely as able-bodied men and women whose physical strength were vital for the development of the continent were taken abroad for slavery. After slave trade was the partitioning of Africa into colonies at the Berlin Conference of 1881 which was basically to divide Africa into colonies for the different European countries. Colonialism emphasized on the exploitation and massive exploration of African natural resources for the development of the mother countries thereby leaving Africa economically and socially undeveloped in spite of the dubious appropriation of its human and natural resources. After colonialism, came neo-colonialism with the wind of freedom and independence that swept across Africa in the early sixties. The foreign colonial powers sought to dominate the economic and political activities in Africa through the use of Africans as surrogates and through the promotion of unfair economic activities that was not in the interest and the overall development of Africa. This they carried out through the prescription of economic policies of doubtful value, through its multi-national agencies like World Bank of IMF and unfair multi-lateral agreements like the General Agreement on Tariffs and Trade (GATT), which seeks to promote the interest of the western world to the detriment of Africa.

2. INTERNAL FACTORS

The internal factors include over-dependence of African leaders on foreign development models and economic policies which of recent have done Africa more harm than good. Most African leaders are surrogates and puppets who are unpopular in their countries but were imposed on the citizenry by the foreign powers for the promotion of their foreign economic interests. Another major internal problem is the deep-rooted corruption and mismanagement which have seen public institutions collapse, public enterprises in shambles, war and social instability on the increase.

Africa needs to look inwards to replace this system of decay with a home-made and internally improvised development model that will ensure sustainable development in Africa.

African Women Development Bank is poised to achieve this goal. According to Walter Rodney in his classical work: "*How Europe underdeveloped Africa*" "African potential is shown to be greater everyday with new discoveries of mineral wealth. On the agricultural side, African soil is not as rich as the picture of tropical forests might lead one to believe; but there are other climatic advantages so that with proper irrigation, crops can be grown all the year round in most parts of the continent"?

With abundance of minerals; metallic and non-metallic, one wonders the reason for this high level of suffering and impoverishment in the continent.

"Africa is well endowed with minerals and primary energy resources. With an estimated nine (9%) percent of the world's population, the region accounts for approximately twenty-eight (28%) percent of the total value of world mineral production and six (16%) percent of its crude petroleum output. In recent years, its share of the latter is increasing.

Of sixteen important metallic and non-metallic minerals, the share of Africa varies from twenty-two (22) to ninety-five (95) percent of the world production" – *United Nations Survey of Economic Conditions in Africa up to 1964.*

The irresponsibility of African leaders has brought great impoverishment and suffering to Africans greater than that of the accumulated years of slavery and colonialism. The height of this irresponsibility is the wanton looting of their respective national wealth and being willing parties to unfair and dubious global trading partnership.

A recent survey by one non-governmental Organization, World Development Movement, shows that income per person in fifty-nine (59) developing countries has fallen over the past fifteen (15) years and that the number of people living on less than US $1 per day has risen significantly during that period. In general terms, these statistics mean that over eight hundred (800) million people are permanently hungry.

On the other hand, the price of commodities on which most developing countries depend for foreign currency earnings, keeps falling. Considering that seven (7) out of ten

(10) people in sub-Saharan Africa depend on agriculture for their livelihood, the bleakness of their welfare becomes glaringly obvious.

Indeed one can imagine the bleakness of the welfare of African women who toil day and night in the farm only for their hard earned agro products to be traded at unfair and dubious prices at world trade markets. Their situation is even more pitiable considering the fact that they are denied agricultural inputs like machines, fertilizers and capital by their governments.

African Women Development Bank should reactivate the industriousness of African women through training, giving of micro-credit and creation of enabling environment for the export of their products at the international market through negotiating tenaciously for a fair global market. This is most crucial given that the third world countries are unfairly treated in international trade arena.

According to John Madelyn in his work: *Trade and the Poor, the Impact of International Trade on Developing Countries: A World Bank publication,* "North-South trade is not taking place between equals, but between a rich bloc and a poor bloc, with the gap between the two growing ever wider.

Throughout the 1980's, the Third World terms of trade – the rate at which exports are exchanged for imports – moved ominously against developing countries. For developed world as a whole the index fell from 100 in 1980 to 75 in 1990, and for Africa it fell to only 68, a drop of over 30 percent in a decade. This means that African countries had to pay out, on average, over 30 percent more in 1989 than they did in 1980 to buy the same quantity of imports. The average figure index shows an even worse situation for some producers".

"Coffee-producing countries for example, were receiving around $500 a ton for the exported raw coffee beans in April 1992, only a small fraction more than in April 1975. But over the same period the prices of some imports of agriculture machinery have risen fivefold.

In 1975, African farmers could have bought a basic tractor for around 8 tons of coffee, in 1992; it would cost them around 40 tons.

"Industrialized countries have generated enough money from their manufactured goods to develop services such as transport fleets, banking and insurance, which again are in growing demand. So these countries are in much stronger trading position than countries whose economies are based on primary produce. And in practice, over the last 40 years or more, the price of manufactured goods have increased faster than price of primary goods. "About half of the foreign earnings, from merchandise of non-oil-producing developing countries come from sales of one or more primary commodity, usually agricultural but also from minerals such as copper. Over the past 30 years, the prices of the great majority of these commodities have been low and unstable. Attempts to develop international commodity agreements have come too little, while attempts to diversify into producing manufactured goods for export had ran into problems both domestic and external.

"Protectionist barriers imposed by western countries make it difficult for the developing world to branch out into manufactured goods. The west employs not only tariffs, which raise the price of imports, but also a growing range of non-tariff barriers. The 1991 World Development Report says that use of protective measures such as quotas, subsidies and voluntary export restraints has risen alarmingly since the 1960's.

"A small number of developing countries have gained economically from international trade and have done so in a quite spectacular manner. The gang of four' – Hong Kong, South Korea, Taiwan, Singapore – have made tremendous economic strides since the early 1960's. They have done so mainly to manufactured goods and by developing the comparative advantage of their work force –which were nonetheless paid low wages and often denied labour rights. The four countries began with garments and textiles and progressed through a variety of miscellaneous products to electronic components; in the seventies the degree of sophistication in the commodities exported increased steadily."

"Between 1964 and 1973, the four countries grew at 10 percent a year and between 1974 and 1983 at 8 percent a year. The barriers that were imposed against many of their goods hindered but did not stop their progress. Once they had taken a step out of poverty and have a foot on the ladder, they continued to climb, even if the climb becomes steeper. The geographical closeness of the four countries to Japan and China undoubtedly helped. And they were helped by being comparatively small countries, (their joint population in 1989 was around 70 million people, only three-quarters of Nigeria's) producing goods that the outside world could just about cope with some restrictions".

"Most of the developing world find it difficult to follow the route of the "gang of four" many Latin American countries have tried but not succeeded with export led policies. Neither the investment nor the domestic purchasing exits for all Third world countries lead to industrialize and market manufactured goods in the way the gang of four have done. There are however; some openings which can be exploited…" these openings that can be exploited in the African context centers on the economic empowerment of African Women through the establishment of African Women development bank. This development will trigger off rural industrialization, cash crop production in large quantities, organized advocacy and international solidarity for better trade deals for Africa at global trade arena and meaningful management of state resources. These opening that can be exploited in the African context center on the economic empowerment of African women through a resolute commitment to the empowerment of

Women whom the circumstance of their culture and social setting have given the burden of creation of goods and services and the maintenance and nature of upcoming African generation.

At the zenith of the developmental crises plaguing the continent is the fact that the life and meaningful existence of too numerous people, children, young boys and girls and even the old depends on the care and maintenance of women. Education, good health, care and feeding of these people are determined by the strength and industriousness of the women. If such women are disenfranchised economically all these dependents are doomed! This is the case in Africa, presently.

When rural women are toiling and suffering, ignorant and greedy men are busy in cities in Africa causing anguish and death through their unbridled mismanagement, corruption and unquenchable thirst for power which increase distrust, instability, war and wanton destruction of human life and properties.

African Women must be empowered economically, politically, and then the renaissance of Africa will emerge and blossom. Anything short of this is mere wishful thinking. The present crop of irresponsible leaders, war mongers, money launderers cannot salvage African economy. Political empowerment must go to that segment of African humanity that use it for the benefit of all. This can be done through a wholesome replacement of the present development approach with an African-oriented one and ensuring the full economic empowerment of African women.

A practical approach towards economic empowerment of African women is the development of a Bank that will propel the disbursement of fund to those who need it. This had already been observed by the report of the South Commission, an association of the heads of governments of developing countries.

"Developing countries in a stronger financial position have an obligation to help the more needy members of the south family. The African bank is an example of this spirit of solidarity in action. Set up by the summit of the non-aligned countries in Harare in September 1986, the AFRICA BANK has so far raised more than $500 million to be devoted to assisting the front-line states and liberation movements in South Africa in their struggle against the Pretoria regime. The successful launch of the AFRICA BANK is an illustration of the South's potential as well as the goodwill that existed within South and within some countries in the North which have made contributions to the fund and its example should encourage the establishment of other multilateral financial schemes for providing assistance to the needy countries".

Africa needs a practical demonstration of ensuring that money should go to those who need it. African women earnestly need money, as they control the industrial and service sectors of the African society. The economic empowerment of African women is a sane road to Africa renaissance. Economic empowerment brings political empowerment and the full restoration of the human rights of an individual thereby propelling such individual to greater productivity and maximum utilization of his or her skill and potential for his or her self-improvement as well as the society she finds herself.

The IMF June 2001 publication-International Economic Policy Review (IEPR) first paper, part 1 "Economic Growth, Inflation, and Poverty", argues that sub-Saharan African's unsatisfactory growth performance, the root of the region's low standard of living and widespread poverty, is due to economic distortions and institutional deficiencies that have scared off potential investors and depressed total factor productivity growth.

Guy Pfefferman writing under the topic – poverty reduction in developing countries, the role of private enterprises in a growing economy. "In almost all developing countries including China household income and expenditure surveys, show that the total number of persons whose incomes are less than $365 a year worldwide –those the World Bank calls the "absolute poor" has not changed much since 1987. Considering the efforts made by governments and aids organizations, the stagnation of the very lowest incomes is disappointing and seems to indicate that no progress has been made in reducing poverty. However, since 1987, the population of those hiring above absolute poverty in developing countries has increased by about one million people. It follows that the number of persons living above absolute poverty line has increased very substantially during the last 15 years; these persons either had never been among the "absolute poor". Examining how one billion people in the developing world stayed out of poverty or escaped it should teach us a lot about what is necessary to achieve large scale poverty reduction.

Guy Pfefferman went further to ask a question. 'How do people manage to escape absolute poverty?' According to him and in fact correctly, "some of the events most closely related to economic improvement are finding a job, or a relative finding a better job, or moving to a better job. Indeed, job creation is a major, probably a major path out of poverty reduction. The most sustainable job creation is by firms, whether they are new and very small or large production units expanding as a private enterprise are the main source of new jobs. These include firms in sectors of activity, large and small firms, domestic to foreign firms, although government job also contribute to income mobility, attempts at deliberate job creation, whether by central government or by State-owned enterprises have nearly always been unsustainable. Public enterprises tend to lose money eventually; many either collapse or become a drain on public resources".

In the context of Africa, the pitiable and lamentable destruction and tacit demolition of social structures and infrastructures worsen the impoverishment of the Africa humanity, particularly women and children. It is women, though, not involved in this reign of institutional destruction that suffers most. They usually bear the consequences of all state mismanagement of human and material resources. It is therefore imperative to note that meaningful socio-economic reform could be attained in Africa if the very important position of women in the African socio-cultural setting is deeply appreciated. Such a reform must aim at the economic empowerment of women who will then be energized to play a zealous and sustainable role towards African economic and social rebirth in the new global order. Hence the urgent and crucial need for the establishment of AFRICAN WOMEN DEVELOPMENT BANK.

It is imperative judging from recent developments in the world financial sector that African women should vigorously pursue the establishment of an autonomous financial institution that should ensure the equitable and honest utilization of such finance realized locally and internationally for meaningful development. Particularly now that the culpability of International Monetary Fund (IMF) and World Bank in the wanton looting of public finance into private banks in western countries have become glaring. Rose Umoren writing on the topic "Recover our loot" on Business in Africa Magazine, November 1999 edition, made the following observation; "More damaging to the banks identity (i.e. World Bank) is Wolfesson declaration on corruption. Where in his letter he pledged support, he now echoed his International Monetary Fund (IMF) colleagues Michel Camdessus, saying that the bank was powerless over banks harbouring monies looted from Nigeria's treasury."

This raises a question about whose interest the bank is serving when its chief shareholders from the United State of America (USA) to Japan are actively assisting in loot recoveries. The answer lies in Wolfesson background as Wall Street Banks personnel who have been actively involved in moving Nigeria's loot around the world. How can the bank which actively trades in the global money market on a daily basis claim inability to influence its bank trading partners. Besides, it uses those banks to move around project and other loans to Nigeria and other third world countries.

The present global financial system in which developing countries mostly from Africa were given financial aid running into hundreds of billions of US dollars, which were later siphoned into private accounts in banks, abroad through the tacit co-operation of the lender is most unfortunate. The resultant consequence is the impoverishment of the citizens particularly women and children. This is a wicked system designed by western creditors and accepted by greedy visionless and irresponsible African leaders. It must be replaced by a responsible, home grown development model. For the past fifty years, New International Economic Orders (NIEO) has created much problem to the Less Developed Countries (LDC).

Instead of economic model prepared and handed over to the African countries by developed countries, alongside economic and development agents such as World Bank and IMF bringing development and progress to Africa, rather it promotes the pauperization of the recipient countries. The glaring misplacement of priority, particularly the empowerment of African women for unproductive and irrelevant jamboree brought to the less developed countries, problems, external reserve depreciation, fluctuation in the prices of their commodities, internal insecurity etc.

Owing to deep seated corruption and lack of vision by governments in Africa and other less developed countries which are male dominate government instead of reducing the gross national product disparities between them and developed countries, they ended up from a growth rate of 5% in 1960-73 to 4.6% in 1974-80, from 4% in 1980 and down to only 2% in 1981; While the developed countries were witnessing tremendous growth in their economy, the less developed recast want inequalities in income per capital to reduce. This has actually worsen since the disparity was 840 dollars for less developed countries, 4640 dollars for Europe, 7030 dollars for USA in 1955, and become 730 dollars for less developed countries, 10.720 dollars for Europe, 9010 dollars for Japan, and 11,560 for the USA in 1980. This shows that the disparity has extended considerably. The less developed countries wanted to reduce fluctuations in the prices of their commodities; instead they witnessed worst fluctuations in the 1980's than they did in the 70s, 80s, 90s and even presently!

The less developed countries wanted to see a reduction in the world reserves of the developed countries and more for them but this was not the case as their original 4% of the total world reserve in the second half of 1970s actually dropped.

In 1975, the less developed countries of sub-Saharan African had an external debt profile of about $18 billion. Twenty years later, the debt burden had risen to over $220 billion. For most of the low and middle-income developing countries, the average ratio of debt was less than 150 percent in 1975. Many countries till date have been unable to service their debt without resources to rescheduling it under Paris Club arrangements or by accumulating arrears due to the highly concessional nature of external financing provided to Africa.

But how did Africa and indeed the black world get itself involved in this deplorable situation? This answer is not farfetched as the result of the irresponsibility and wickedness of corruption and greedy African male dominated leadership and the highly dubious external economic policies.

The less developed countries wanted to reduce the balance of payment deficit in their economies, but unfortunately for Africa, their current account deficit increased from 2.0billion dollars in 1973 to 6.3billion dollars in 1978, to 8.1 dollars in 1976-78 and up to

12.0billion dollars in 1979-1980. Having enmeshed itself in deep economic mess masterminded by corruption and instability of its leaders the less developed countries demanded the developed countries to give them continuous aids of about 0.7% of their GNP's, but they find it difficult to do this except Netherlands and Denmark. The US, Japan, Switzerland, Finland and Australia commit less than 0.3% of their GNPs; these suffocating aid unfortunately comes as loan with killing conditions.

The less-developed countries aspired for a less domination of their economies by the multinational co-operations, unfortunately the multinational co-operation control almost 80% of the economies of the less developed countries.

The less developed countries wanted technology but were give outdated & inappropriate ones or at best guided transferred ones, managed closely by the developed countries. But how can the less developed countries extricate itself from this pitiable vicious circle of retrogression? Obviously the answer lies within. This can be achieved by that segment of Africans that is not corrupt; the African women. African women equipped by their industriousness would guarantee Africa's itself reliance through improved internal production and prudent management.

Therefore African women must be empowered economically by avoiding currencies hoarding, currency speculation and currency protectionism. Money must go to those who need it. African Women Development Bank must serve as a necessary foundation for a meaningful and sustained social Renaissance and progress in Africa.

Chapter Two

Report Of The African Continent

The tour to the countries of the continent assisted us tremendously in knowing the situation of the rural poor, particularly during the tour, we realize that the rural poor do not have access to credit neither do they have job opportunities. Unemployment was common as there were no existence of industries, big, medium or small scale industries. The rural women and children are the major victims of corruption of governments which include huge debt profile as well as war and political instability.

We observed that African rural women posses the ability and organizational strength for the following:

1. Production of farm products for consumption at family and industrial usage.
2. Possess organizational strength for effective co-operative, which encourages the polling of resources together for meaningful projects.
3. Support themselves in the establishment of social infrastructures and services e.g. market stalls, co-operative hall, clinics and maternal centers.
4. Solidarity and effective network vital for economic development.

We observed that these women are industrious, honest, diligent and co-operative. If only they could receive some form of training and some micro-credit they would be able to produce enough for their family and surplus for industrial usage and export. After being turned away by every bank save one in the Ugandan capital Kampala, a small scale rural industrialist formulated a bitter and Universal truth about how traditional banks view the poor: "they were only willing to lend the money if I could prove that I did not need it" this is the unfortunate situation which rural women in the continent face.

The employment of African women is the only way in which their industriousness and courage would be relevant in building a strong and progressive Africa. I am convinced and optimistic that African Women Development Bank will do this. "Poverty alleviation remains today one of the fundamental concerns in the development community and demands the empowerment of the poor in member countries. This empowerment calls for the support and promotion of the self esteem and self supportiveness of the population in depressed area; it especially calls for the promotion of micro-enterprises through access to credit for the acquisition and growth in ownership of productive physical assets by the poor as well as the productivity of these assets."

Presently, the absence of financial institutions and establishments devoted solely to this cause is a serious concern to the actualization of the dream of complete economic empowerment. On information and communication, the rural women are much left out, as they are grappling with mere effort to survive. They concentrate with the daily toiling and struggling in the farm. The governments of respective countries have not helped matters as everything that is necessary to nurture Information Technology (IT) revolution is in pitifully short supply in the countries, including telephone lines, electricity, affordable computers, education, literacy, housing and vibrant economy. In Nigeria a Private computer cost ten (10) times the average annual income. In sub-Saharan Africa only 43% of the population has access to the internet. Strong as communication is in poverty alleviation. This is where African Women Development Bank will play a very vital role; empowering women to empower themselves through modern technological advancement.

Most unfortunately, we discovered the African's burden: the debt trap.

We discovered that:

In 1980 sub-Saharan Africa owed the West 1bn.While in 1997 this had risen to $357 for every man, women and child on the continent.

The worst affected African countries presently are spending up to 48% of their budgets in servicing the debts, let alone writing off any capital.

- Countries like Zambia, Burkina Faso, Rwanda and Tanzania spend as much on debt servicing as they do on health and education combined. Africa actually repays $14.4bn annually to the west, which is twice what African Countries can afford to pay on health care.

- In 1996 Africa paid more to their creditors than it received in aid. For every $1 that Africa receives in aid, it pays back $1 .3 in dept service.

- Many African countries find out that they cannot pay off all the interest on their depts. In other words, they cannot keep up with the dept servicing let alone bring down the total value of the debt that they owe.

- Some African countries are so proud they simply cannot keep up with debt repayment.

THE SAD INVOLVEMENT OF AFRICAN GOVERNMENT IN CORRUPTION

Of the monumental sum of money, about eight trillion dollars, borrowed by African Governments from World Bank and other financial institutions only about 20% reached Africa. More than 80% of these loans mostly acquired in 1980s went instead into private bank accounts in Europe and America.

According to Mr. Sail Shetty, head of the Millennium Development Goal Unit at the United Nations, Africa requires an additional $50 billion (abut N6.4trillion) to meet the Millennium Development Goal of reducing poverty by half in 2015.

- The Millennium Development Goals, as agreed to by the international community in September 2000, aim to reduce poverty by 2015 and spur big improvement in education, gender equality and health care; the goals also aim at overcoming hunger and environmental degradation. Unfortunately, only a few sub-Saharan African economies currently grew at an average of about five percent needed to halve poverty by 2015.

- Most African countries use about 60% of their income to purchase arms, often to promote civil unrest in their own domain; women and children are the victims. High rate of corruption and careless spending ensure that the loans they acquire from monetary agencies are kept in private accounts abroad. Governments invest most of the money in political patronage, wasteful jamborees and dubious contracts that were never completed.

- Most countries are involved in civil unrest and bitter internal battle that they spend huge sum of national wealth purchasing ammunition to curb insurrection and uprising, thus leaving them with little or nothing to use in national development.

THE FAMINE IN AFRICA

The famine and drought that is affecting numerous African countries is unfortunate – Africans suffer the scathing effect of famine and drought as a result of mismanagement and insensibility, the most vulnerable group, women and children suffer most.

Presently there is famine in Mali, Mauritania, South African countries of Malawi, Zimbabwe, Somalia and Ethiopia as well as Eriteria all in the horn of Africa. The situation worsened by no provision and structures of food and water distribution as all social services have been grounded. Women and children suffer greatly. A vivid picture of the human degradation going on in Africa can be summarized by the observation of Lara Santon and Jeffery Barshoft in the Newsweek news magazine of April 24, 2000". Badia Omar, whose gleaming white teeth seem almost too pretty for her emaciated body, doesn't know whether her husband is still alive. For months, they wondered together across the parched lowlands of Ethiopia, as thirst and hunger claimed their 200 sheep, 25 cows and one goat, after two of their five children perished, Badia's husband wandered off. "He could not stay and watch the children die. She says together with her three surviving kids and two donkeys, Badia made for the town of Gode in the Ogden region. The donkeys died during the 18-day trek: people told me there would be something here, some food for us, "says Badia, crunched in a corner of a makeshift-feeding center that is made of twigs. Hundreds of other women are waiting here, too many of them abandoned by their husbands. Badia's 1-year Aldi, weights 61 percent of what the doctor's say he ought to. Now he is getting oral dehydration solution which he can barely hold down. The feeding center has food for only the worst cases, however, so Badia has left her two daughters in town to fend for themselves. Badia and her family aren't the only people forced by catastrophe to make hard choices; politicians have far more consequential decisions to make, even if they, personally, have much less to stake. Ethiopia and the surrounding countries in the horn of Africa, known for two of the worst famines in memory are now facing another major food shortage. The United Nations estimates that up to 16millionm people, half of them in Ethiopia need urgent food and medical aid to avert widespread death by starvation. The approximate cause of the disaster is severe drought, which has persisted for three years in some areas. But this natural calamity is compounded by war and by the rivalries, fear and misplaced pride of regional leaders.

The leaders have no pity on the effects of wars, huge military expenditure on the overall development and progress of the society. They instead engage in bitter wars that claim lives of millions of people. Ironically, it is the toil and suffering of the women that produces the cash crops that create the foreign exchange for the purchase of these weapons of mass destruction. Women who toil day and night in sustaining the economic life of the nations are deprived education, training, health care, social amenities, instead of being encouraged they receive terror, fear, insecurity and death. There is an urgent need for a reformation. The marginalization of women in socio-political affairs in e continent must stop.

Shamefully, almost all the parliaments, ranging from local to national assembly situated at the capital cities of sovereign states in Africa, are all dominated by men, these law making halls are men dominated gathering where the emphasis is on who gets what and how. No wonder these visionless law makers are accessories to wanton looting of national treasuries of their various countries. None of them care for the welfare of the message, particularly women and children.

Women having been shortchanged in the economic distribution in their respective countries have no economic base to contest for responsible positions.

They consequently become helpless victims of shameless, heartless money mongers that parade the corridors of power across the capital cities in Africa. The outcome of this pitiable situation is series of wars, destruction and wanton depravity and poverty.

The law makers are mostly busy talking about "budgets", money allocation for this, allocation for that of which in the final analysis no effective monitoring is instituted to find out how the money is being spent or at least whether it goes into the projects and programmes for which they were made.

This cheat-as-you-can attitude, this lack of accountability, and focus by public officers, unfortunately is the dominating factor militating against African development. Worst still African women who are the pivot of economic and social development are denied all access to finance, equipment, education, skill and training through useless policies of dubious and irresponsible governments; Thus making life more tasking and miserable for the vulnerable group, mothers and their children.

THE STRUCTURAL ADJUSTMENT PROGRAMME ALBATROSS

The irresponsibility of African leaders is glaringly exemplifies by the shortsighted policy that came with the questionable loans they received from countries and donor agencies as well as banks goes together with very destructive consequences to the welfare and social development of the citizens particularly the women, such policies like the Structural Adjustment Programme have reduced social infrastructure to rubbles, increase consumer products, reduced government responsibility to subsidized educational, health and agricultural sectors. But ensure increase in interest rate of bank lending, scarcity of foreign exchange, huge military spending, low export and huge import spending thus causing astronomical trade deficit. In all, capital flow is restricted to the looters at the corridors of power.

In both instances, women were totally excluded they lack the economic base required in these projects. The projects are mostly hijacked by those men who have milked the country dry at one time or the other in the cause of their national and public engagement.

Majority of the women in Nigeria go through bitter agony and pain to feed their children in worsening economic environment; The worst agony being the brazen state of insecurity presently being promoted by men in the mad quest for power and wealth; extra judicial killing by government, politically motivated assassinations, ritual killings, rape, arson, assaults are now rife, while armed robbery, bomb explosion increased the fear of the weak and accelerated death out of fear and frustration.

In the melee of anarchy, change almost seem impossible as solidarity and advocacy is weak owing to the fact that women are presently grappling with the challenge of what to eat and where to put their head. To liberate them from this chain of wickedness, efforts must be made for their economic empowerment. This requires the urgent provision of education, information, skill and finance to them for their total development and by extension, the development of Nigeria: money must reach those who need it. This is the challenge of African Women Development Bank on-line.

INCREASE IN PREVENTABLE AND CURABLE DISEASES

Regrettably rural African women and children are still plagued by preventable and curable diseases. Diseases such as malaria, typhoid, tuberculosis and the dreaded HIV/AIDS coupled with malnutrition have led to many deaths in recent times. Malaria kills over one million people world-wide every year and most of these preventable deaths are among African children. Malaria accounts for 20 percent of infant mortality in Africa and compromises 10 percent of the continent's overall disease burden.

In rural Africa, we discovered that malaria causes 30-50 percent if in admissions, 40 percent of the public health expenditures and up to 50 percent of outpatient visits in malaria areas. It causes anemia and also increase risk of miscarriage and is responsible for low child development.

We discovered with total dismay that malaria remains one of the major obstacles to development in Africa.

- Africa's GDP would be up to $100 billion greater today if malaria had been eliminated 35 years ago.
- In Africa, malaria continues to slow down economic growth by more than one percent of GDP.
- Malaria endemic countries are among the world's most impoverished.
- A Malaria-stricken family spends an average of over one quarter of its income on malaria treatment as well as paying prevention costs and suffering loss of income.
- Malaria impairs learning in children living in endemic areas and is a major cause of school absenteeism.
- Malaria, one through to be conquered is present ravaging lives in rural African.

Another major disease ravaging rural Africa of which women and children are the worst hit is the deadly HIV/AIDS scourge".

More than 12 million children in sub-Saharan Africa have been orphaned by AIDS. Villages are becoming ghost towns, local economies are curbing, the orphaned children, as adults will not require to drive the economic engine of Africa. This will make the struggle for development and growth on the continent even tougher.

Tuberculosis cases are increasing by 10% a year in Africa because of HIV/AIDS. There were nearly 2 million near TB cases in Africa in 1999, with two thirds of those also infected with HIV. It is estimated that the number of TB cases in Africa will reach 3.3 million by 2005 and surpass 4 million soon after. The most affected in this ugly trend being women and children, they women urgently need economic empowerment as deep sited poverty, squalor and malnutrition sustains the wide spread of these disease.

While women and children are dying as a result of deadly disease, polluted water and poor nutrition, African government and donor countries are busy organizing deceptive conferences as jamborees that result to nothing.

LAMENTABLE RATE OF CORRUPTION AND MISMANAGEMENT

From our investigation we discovered with deep regret that most public officers embezzle public fund on an alarming scale there by leaving most countries further impoverished. An example is the Nigerian case, since independence in 1960; Nigeria has lost about $600 billion to private pockets. There is a monumental thievery in government and public circle which have frustrated all effort at meaningful development. As of present Nigeria is one of 34 sub-Saharan African growth and opportunity act countries to export their products under a fair trade agreement to the united states, e.g. United States apparel market is worth over $80 billion a year. By Nigeria involvement in exporting clothing to the U.S. it will boast its non-oil export, but this could only be achieved if the government empowers its citizens through training, skill acquisition and accessibility to credit facilities; particularly women who dominate the industrial and service sector of the downstream economy.

Deep-sited corruptions have increased the collapse of social services and infrastructures such as electricity, Tele-communication, road networks and fuel distribution. There is also a lot of forgery going on at the ports which frustrate genuine trade and transactions but enrich corrupt custom officials. All these add to the worsening economic situation of the engine room of African Development – the women.

HIGH INCIDENT OF MATERNAL DEATH AND INFANT MORTALITY IN RURAL AFRICA

"No country sends to war it's men to protect their country without seeing to it that they will return safely and yet mankind for centuries has been sending women to battle to renew the human resource without protecting them" - Fred Sai, former President of the international planned parenthood federation. Owing to high rate of inflation, decayed social infrastructure and services including hospital, women seldom get desired attention they earnestly need during pregnancy. This detestable state of affairs has made child bearing a very difficult task for rural African women. Sub-Saharan Africa records the highest incident of high mortality in the world. 1 in 3 women dies of pregnancy-related causes during her lifetime compared to other parts of the world.

"Tragically, these deaths are just part of the picture, for every woman who die, approximately 30 more women suffer injuries, infection and disabilities during pregnancy or child-birth, at least 15 million women a year. The cumulative total of those affected has been estimated at 300 million or more than quarter of adult women in the developing world. These pregnancy –related health problem include severe anemia, infertility and damage to the uterus and reproductive tract sustained during childbirth. Obstetric fistula (tear between the virgina and the urinary tract or rectum that causes permanent incontinence if not treated) are especially devastating. Many women are too ashamed to speak about these and other conditions or to seek treatment for them. This "Culture of Silence" is exacerbated in a setting where women are not empowered to make choices and act freely to take care of their health.

Maternal mortality in 1995, as estimated by WHO, UNICEF and UNFPA, shows the inability of government in African to provide essential services and infrastructure vital for the safety of women during pregnancy and delivery. Thus highlighting the detestable state of economic disempowerment of African women by callous and irresponsible governments which have made child delivery and motherhood a nigh mare in sub-

Saharan Africa, "Maternal mortality is influenced by the social, economic and political context of the health care system and the cultural and biological realities of women seeking care. This complex interaction means that even when skilled care is available, women may not seek it out or receive it. At several stages of the journey through pregnancy and child birth, women face delay in receiving skilled care. These delays pose barriers to safe motherhood. Women and their families or caregivers may not recognize the warning signs of life-threatening complications; women may have difficulty reaching a decision to seek medical care; they may fear rude treatment, high fees, or substandard care at health facilities. Women may also fail delays in reaching health facilities in time. Even deliveries in health facilities may be needlessly risky because of poor quality obstetric care and the lack of medical supplies of blood. These delays are interrelated and reflect a country's level of Socio-economic development. Maternal mortality in 1995: estimated development by; WHO, UNICEF and UNEPA.

Incidents of reoccurring maternal death have caused deep anguish in many families in rural Africa as it affects the economic and social development of a large number of dependents on the affected women because the vast majority of women who die or are seriously injured are in the prime of life, their illnesses and deaths have dire social and economic consequences for both families and communities. Families forgo a women's crucial role in household management and care for children and other family members. Consequently, families that lose mothers are likely to suffer declining nutritional status. Surviving children may have lower rates of school enrollment, maternal disabilities related to pregnancy and childbirth, such as anemia and malnutrition also influence child birth health. Babies born to malnourished mothers are more likely to have low birth weights, which are associated with development delays, disabilities and early death.

THE AGGREGATE EFFORTS TOWARDS SUSTAINABLE DEVELOPMENT BY WOMEN

Almost in all rural villages we visited, women were the pivot of social and economic life through their enterprise in rural agriculture and trading. They do most of the work in the farm and in most cases supplement their efforts in agriculture with petty trading to fend for the family.

In few cases where their husbands are enterprising it is because of the reliability, motivation and support such men receive from their wives, through their assistance, motivation and direct involvement, which enhances Family income and development.

Unfortunately, the same women are denied the right to inherit the properties of their husbands in the case of death. Instead of the women being in charge of what belongs to them, they were subjected to humiliating, agonizing, terrible cultural practices; particularly the widowhood practices which is prevalent among tribes in southern Nigeria.

Under the widowhood practices, the bereaved women went through a lot of trauma which involves her bathing with the same water left from the washing of her late husband and in most cases total starvation for many days.

These practices unfortunately are going on among native tribes in rural Africa even now. Amidst the terror, torture and deprivation that the rural African women go in through and are in most cases subjected to, they are still the goose that lay the golden egg. One could only imagine the level of development that Africa will witness if this "goose acquire the training, gain access to credit, have right to acquire and own property and have access to social amenities.

Presently amidst towering handicaps, rural African women still engage in the production of goods and services, they grow agricultural products that serve as food for the teaming population and cash crops for foreign exchange. They engage in storage of this products, distribution of food through rural and urban markets, as well as to the relevant Agro-industries. Yet they denied capital, agricultural inputs, irrigation facilities, social amenities in return for their great efforts and sacrifice.

We saw nothing in all rural African to justify the huge capital and technical facilities which countries receive from donor agencies. Instead we saw women with crude implements, little or no technical knowhow and total denial of even micro-credit. Somewhere in the Horn of Africa, Ethiopia under the leadership of President MelesZanawi, spend an estimated $1,000, 000 every day to wage war against Eritrea over a barren town of no strategic value and coupled with the present horrible famine and draught that is ravaging the country.

Unfortunately, donor agencies keep on channeling their financial aid to these irresponsible leaders, thereby tacitly endorsing and encouraging wars and misery in Africa. There is unarguably a need for a reform. African Women Development Bank is the answer.

WAR, VIOLENCE AND POLITICAL INSTABILITY IN AFRICA

With great dismay we discovered that the greatest factor sustaining bitter wars in African countries are the great quest forthe exploitation and acquisition of wealth from natural resources in various countries. Countries such as Sierra Leone, Liberia, Guinea, Sudan, Uganda, Somalia, Congo Republic, Angola, Rwanda, Burundi are bitterly engaged in deadly civil strife that have led to the death of numerous citizens particularly mothers and their children.

While the scramble for the control of natural wealth derived from minerals such as Diamond, Gold, Petroleum, Copper, Zinc, Iron, Uranium, motivated the bitter rivalry that existed among the European colonialists, during the scramble and partitioning of Africa, modern Africa Statesmen unfortunately are greedily engage in looting and misapplication of wealth derived from the huge deposit of natural resources in Africa. It is the greed of man as exhibited by the desire to be at power at all cost that sustained the spate of bloodletting and bitter wars around Africa since the independence of most nations in the early 60's.

It is inevitable and most crucial, at this point of the continents' quest for a rebirth, I remember vividly a particular case that happened in a village in Liberia where we were treated to a pitiable picture of the appalling fate of the African women and their children over wars and political conflict caused and sustained by the greed and corruption of men.

In Liberia according to a commonly leader in a rural village south east of Monrovia, "we have migrated to eight locations since the commencement of this war; most of us have lost our young male children in this bitter combat that we do not know what it is all about. We suffer a lot in the hands of the soldiers, they strike unannounced, dragging us out, rape us and cart away all our farm produce. We are hungry, we are not at peace, and we are at the mercy of bullet, particularly we that live near the mining area.

WHAT WARS HAVE DONE TO AFRICA

Wars have retarded the progress of Africa, destroyed the work force, retard economic progress and promoted misery, squalor, want, hunger and death. It is a pitiable scene to behold, where old and young women were raped, disfigured and at times killed; atrocities all committed by men. In all these wickedness it is Africa men that are responsible.By their greed and lack of vision they have collectively set back race and enshrined an experience of poverty, wants and shame in the continent. In all this milee of wickedness and monstrous confusion, women were not involved. In all the war, women were not culpable! only the men! It is the men! Therefore it is time authority; power and leadership are taken from them to enable Africa experience peace for a while.

THE AMPUTATION OF CITIZENS

A visit to the Aberdeen Road Amputee Camp in Freetown will amplify the reality of the irresponsibility of contemporary leaders in Africa and the urgent need to address the contemporary state of functional lawlessness.

In Sierra Leone –Aberdeen Road, Amputee Camp, Lamin Ahmed 40, Michael Koroma, 39, KogonaIsmaila, 42 and little Miss Abigail, 14 narrated their stories as they were mercilessly disfigured by rebel Soldier to the extent that they have to vote in an election to produce a new President in their country with their toes because their arms were hacked off during the war.

According to Abigail, "I won't forget how they raped both of us and later killed our mother., My mother was very loving and kind ordering that I and my sister should come out, my mother maintained that there is no young girls around. But the monsters still over ran us, as we all sneak out through the back door to the bush. Their random shooting terrified us to surrender our tender body under a tree where they finally descended on us, raping all of us, taking along my other senior sisters and chopped of my hands. I lay there unconscious until I later realized that they raped and killed our mother".

In rural market in Angola about sixty percent of all the women that were present were aided with crutches, they either have one of their legs chopped off or their limbs hacked off. About seventy percent of farm lands in that country are endangered by land mines planted by warring factions engaged in the over twenty years civil war. Let us not tail about the ethnic cleansing in Rwanda and Burundi involving the Hutus and Tutsis; the horrendous accounts are legion, we can go on and on but that will not help the situation, what is vital is the extrication of Africa from the mess. The major step is toward empowering that segment of African humanity that is totally free of all thesedreat crimes against humanity prevalent in Africa. The first and vital empowerment must be economic and the recipients must be women! They are the hope of Africa contemporarily, not a mad, greedy lot that are occupied with killing, destruction and looting.

FOREIGN DIRECT INVESTMENT

We discover that foreign direct investment has a dynamic and growing source of capital flow to developing countries in recent years, FDI net flows to developing countries increased from $500 million in 1965 to slightly over $10 billion in 1985 and then more than triple, to almost $34billion in 1991. Until the mid 1970's the level of Foreign Direct Investment in sub-Saharan Africa was similar to that of other developing regions. In the 1980's, however, there was a marked decline and FDI now plays a small role in overall investment and total external resource flows.

In the period of, 1977 to 1997, the share of African countries in total Foreign Direct Investment (FDI) flows to developing countries has remained stagnate at $1.3billion. Nigeria is the only country which has attracted large sum of FDI, mainly for its oil and gas sector.

Sadly, we discovered that this great decline in the FDI is as a result of lack of trust on the political and economic environment of African countries by foreign entrepreneurs. Most countries are enmeshed in bitter internal crises, ethnic suspicion and bitter political battle. Equally deep sited corruption, lack of transparency, accountability and outright looting of the national treasury. This unfortunate event has brought a devastating consequence in its wake of which the major culprits are men while the victims are women.

ECONOMIC DISEMPOWERMENT AND SOCIAL MARGINALIZATION

We sadly discovered that 98% of rural African women are living on less than $1 a day, by World Bank Standard, below poverty line. Most of them are engaged in petty trading and subsistence agriculture while many are labourers and manual workers in plantations, mines and industries where they were exploited, marginalized, abused and dehumanized.

The disequilibrium in the allocation of national wealth between men and women were so glaring in most countries owing to age-long marginalization that have been entrenched and accepted by the society particularly – inability of women to inherit property,acquire land and obtain loans and credit from financial institutions. The economic disempowerment of women manifests itself on the economic alienation and disfranchisement of women in the economic sectors of different African countries. Owing to inability of women to obtain financial support from financial institutions and markets, their industry and initiative are frustrated,thereby excluding them from main economic stream of the countries, the resultant effect of this detestable social syndrome is that women are not involved in the ownership of big co-operations and financial institution while their sole proprietorship in some cases are only for the sustenance of their immediate family.

Unfortunately, while women dominate the micro economic sectors of different countries through their activities in rural farming plantation, agriculture, household goods production, agricultural raw materials processing, preservation and storage of farm products as well as maintenance of stable family and preservation of wholesome and reasonable social values, the selfishness and greediness of man exclude them glaringly in the management of the macro economic sectors of the economy of respective nations thus, frustrating, that segment of humanity whose activities sustain the social and economic life of the state, frustrate growth and promote impoverishment invariably. This is the unfortunate case in Africa.

We found out that the huge debt trap at the neck of the continent at the present is as a result of mismanagement, decayed value system and deep rooted corruption initiated and sustained by men. All over Africa, it is men that negotiated and are negotiating, initiated and are initiating, executed dubiously and are executing dubiously when it comes to loan acquisition, initiation of policies of doubtful value and execution of ridiculous and deeply corrupt projects. Women are not involved in this chain of bondage and mess, never! In all the countries we visited, we do not have any cause or evidence to accuse women of involvement in this mess.

How can women work so hard and earn so little?, In Africa, the political and economic marginalization as well as cultural and social victimization of women negates universal value system. This is the bane of Africa. The ambitious and wicked domination of men have resulted in the pauperization of women and by extension the African humanity. I am convinced that of the nearly 320 billion of dollar owed the world financial institutions by African countries, if 1/3 were managed and utilized by women the story could have been different in Africa today; Hence the need for an autonomous financial body that will sponsor women and champion the clamour for their economic independence.

THE LAMENTABLE DECAY IN THE EDUCATIONAL SECTOR

A major sector that has greatly been affected by the present societal decay and development crises in Africa is the educational sector. Pitiably, education which is unarguably the instrument that is vital for African physical and conscious emancipation as well as renaissance has been a major victim of vision-less leadership in Africa.

May I summarize our observation by citing extensively a similar observation made in the West African magazine issue no. 4206 December 1999; "Education in Africa has literally collapsed everywhere. Academic standards are low, children learn in ramshackle classrooms, school teachers and college lecturers are, violent and all too ready to give up their studies for a day out in the streets. Drop outs have given up tutorials for an early place on the lengthening unemployment queues"

"The causes of this debacle are many, armed conflicts, lack of continuity in policies, economic pressures, bad governance, debt, structural adjustment policies, student unrest and traditional resistance to western education". "Nowhere has collapse of education been more alarming than conflict area like Rwanda, Uganda, Sudan, Somalia, Sierra Leone, Liberia, Chad and Angola".

'As Liberia struggles to settle into formal education after a brutal civil war that lasted eight years, only 35 percent of its people are thought to be able to read and write. In a society that saw pre-teenage and early teenage boys coerced into war-front where shooting and killing as everyday action were common. At any rate, poorly staffed and equipped schools are more likely to defer learning than encourage it. Veteran educationist, Lucy

Cole says. "Nowadays, young people are more interested in making a living than go to school".

In Sierra Lone, the toll of the armed struggle between rebel and government forces has been equally devastating for the educational system. Schools were closed and classes were frequently disrupted where they were open. "The situation was worsened by the fact that in venting their anger on the educated class, rebel action targeted pupils and students, easily grouping them with the enemy. The streets of Freetown and other urban population centers are filled with displaced children, victims of the war, their limbs amputated, roaming the roadways begging for alms. They should be in school.

"Even before the war, for every 100, 000 children starting school, only 10,000 reached the fifth form and 2,000 went on to tertiary education. Today about 40 percent of children of school age are not receiving formal education. It does not go well for Sierra Leone's recovery and it is another statistic showing how Africa is deferred in the race to catch up with the rest of the world. "The protracted decline in African economies is a major contribution to the crises in education. Debt repayments have aggravated an already difficult condition.

"Following the two major oil crises in 1973 and 1979 compounded by the fall in export earnings, several African countries slid into and listed among the world's poorest, add to this fact, they spend as much on debt repayment as they jointly on health and basic education. $12billion in 1996, according to World Bank figures, consider also that per capital spending is today less than half of what it was in 1980. Tanzania, that has good record on education in Africa, illustrates the point. It spends six times more on debt replacement than on education. "Although the fall in education began earlier, the spectacular collapse so evident today started in earnest in the 1990s. It arose in the aftermath of a decade long period of structural adjustment policies implemented by the International Monetary Fund (IMF) and under the guidance of the World Bank. Statistics are clear indications of what transpired.

The rate of education was at only 25 percent in 1960. It rose to nearly 60 percent by 1980. School enrolment began to fall in the mid 1980's although this later recovered to hold at around the earlier figure of 60 percent but these figures do not tell the full story of the real state of primary education. In Niger, poorest among the poorest nations in Africa, 70 percent of children old enough are not in school. The rate of illiteracy is at a staggering 83 percent in a country with 50 percent of the population under the age of 15.

In Burkina Faso, only nine percent of women over the age of 15 are literate, only 24 percent of primary school age girls are enrolled. "On average, not less than one-third of children enrolled in primary schools in Africa drop out before the fifth grade, this means that 40million schools age children are today not in the system. Only 60 percent of boys and 51 percent of girls enrolled in primary schools in sub-Saharan Africa". I cannot go further for this endless story of woe is frustrating. The major victim of callous and mindless looting and destruction of human and material resources in Africa are women and children by denying young generations' qualitative education, what next is left of Africa? But who is responsible for this wicked state of affairs? Obviously, African leaders, Western donor agencies and their financial assistance of doubtful value.

Watching teenagers being conscripted as soldiers, watching amputated young boys and girls begging in the streets of major town and cities watching little boys and girls studying under trees, gives one great worry and concern over the present crop of leaders and development model obtainable in Africa. Unarguably, the present system must be replaced, both in theory and in practice if Africa must catch up with other contenders in the global family. We are convinced that the economic empowerment of African women is the answer.

Contemporarily, most young girls who should be in school or employed in the industries are falling victim of female trafficking syndicates who trade them in Europe for economic gain. These young girls go through untold debasement of the dignity of womanhood through torture, sexual exploitation, mating with animals, working in plantation, leaving them with disease, psychologically tortured, socially segregated and death by installment. The root cause of this detested state of affair being bad development policies and faceless, visionless leaders. There is an urgent need for a reform. The major reform being that money must go to those who need it; the contemporary development model project that will ensure unrestricted flow of capital from donors to those who need it. A situation where a few people embezzle monumental amount made for national development while the poor suffer is unacceptable.

VICTIMS OF THESE CHAINS OF IRRESPONSIBILITES

The major victim of this irresponsibility and wickedness by African governments are women and children, they are not involved in the negotiation stage before the acquisition of the loan, and they were not engaged in the development of policies and projects. Yet they suffer greatly from the irresponsible, greed and corrupt practices of these wicked and faceless governments. The faceless predators with their local and foreign collaborators need not frustrate their humble clamour for a meaningful existence anymore.

With every sense of honesty and sincerity, money should go straight to those who need it. Social services and infrastructure should be put in place, maintained and enjoyed by those who sincerely need them; African women being in the forefront of agricultural and industrial development need unrestrained access to training and capital. This must be done through a radical, well thought out development model that would ensure that money, training, information must go to those who dearly need them; the African women.

We discovered with stern clarity and conviction that the inability of policy makers and development institutions to improvise a means through which money can go directly to those who need it at the right time is the bane of Africa and the major sustenance of its underdevelopment.

TOUR OF THE AFRICAN CONTINENT: THE NIGERIA EXPERIENCE

In Nigeria, we witnessed in its totality, the brutal, negligent, corrupt and social approach decay that has chained Africa for a long time. We saw in Nigeria, a sleeping giant; the ninth oil producing nation with the tenth largest gas reserve in the world but yet the thirteen poorest country and second most corrupt country in the world.

In Nigeria we witnessed bitter ethnic and religious tension being exacerbated by wicked retrogressive and greedy members of the political class for selfish reason and interest. In Nigeria, we saw the total collapse of virtually all the social Infrastructures, Hospitals, Electricity, Schools, Roads, Communication and portable water.

In Nigeria, we saw sky rise buildings and magnificent personal residence in cities as well as posh cars and exotic resorts and gardens situated by the side of deep squalor, and squalid environment where most households live without good drinking water, without electricity and communication facilities or food to eat.

In Nigeria, we saw numerous uncompleted projects, huge projects vital for the economic and social development of the country such as the Ajaokuta Steel complex, the Aluminum extraction plant at IkotObasi, numerous industries and other projects like specialist hospitals, major project sites, vital industries, research and development projects all abandoned most pitiably, they were all initiated with loan acquired from abroad.

In Nigeria, we saw a plethora of banks and financial institutions, yet there was total collapse of the industrial sector, unemployment and wide spread hunger and squalor. Ironically, the huge end of the year profit being declared by the banks were rubbished by all time high inflation, foreign exchange speculation, currencyhauling and all time money laundering.

In Nigeria, we saw a government that publicly declared that it is committed to fighting corruption and even went ahead to set up an anti-corruption commission being labeled the second most corrupt government in the world. In Nigeria, we found a country in which some citizens are richer than the state. We found a country of unrestricted looting of public fund by officers.

In Nigeria, we found a country where corruption is so deeply entrenched that the leaders lack any moral persuasion or strength to enforce any meaningful social cleansing.

In Nigeria, we found a country where tribalism, and religion fanaticism is celebrated to the detriment of collective development.

In Nigeria, we found a country in which an old, corrupt and irresponsible mafia tenaciously hold firm to power and economic resources. This was aptly captured by MobalajiSanusi in his write up in the Vanguard Newspaper of September 6, 2002. He observed "At the inception of the Fourth Republic, the word "recycle" become so popular. It was a derisive epithet for describing the present administrations penchant for appointing very old failures of yester years to public office. The not-so impressive performances of the present older patriots that contributed to the failure of past administration were immense."

THE ALARMING RATE OF MARGINALIZATION AND VIOLENCE AGAINST WOMEN

Perhaps worst in the chronicle of bestiality and social crises in Nigeria is high rate of discrimination and violence against women. Bitter and gruesome barbaric acts like female genital mutilation, economic and political exclusion are rife while the climax of this senseless, cannibalism is the death penalty to the opposite sex. In fact in Sokoto and Katsina states, women would have been stoned to death after being convicted of having sex with men by the religious courts in these states of Nigeria but for public and international outcry.

In the Itsekiri tribe of Southern Nigeria, women were recently brutalized by soldiers at the orders of the state for attempting to demand for some rights from multinational oil corporations involved in oil exploration in their area.

Perhaps the worst case of marginalization among women in this country is the total shameful exclusion of women in the (financial) sector of the country. Almost all the financial institutions and blue chip co-operations that control the economy of the country are dominated and managed by men. Presently, numerous state owned enterprises are being privatized for participation in the provision of communication and energy services.

The debt problem of which women and children are the worst hit is getting out of hands as countries find it extremely difficult to meet up with their responsibility of national development. Yet the responsibility of negotiation, acquisition and the execution of projects with these questionable loans is all responsibilities of men dominated African governments, no single woman was involved; yet women and children are paying the great price.

The situation is becoming so frightening that domestic products had been falling totally while earnings from export almost go into debt servicing leaving major areas of national development, housing, agriculture, health, education, road construction, electricity and telecommunication as well as education to suffer. This pitiable situation can be further illustrated by comparing the total exporting debt profile of such countries with the total exporting earnings of such countries from 1994-96, thereby working out their percentage equivalent.

COUNTRIES	DEBT AS % OF EXPORT EARNINGS		
	1994- 96 1996	TOTAL DEBT	US$ IN BN,
Somalia	3,671	2.6	
Guinea-Bissau	3,509	0.9	
Soa Tome Principe	2,132	0.2	
Sudan	2,131	16.9	
Mozambique	1,411	5.8	
Ethiopia	1,377	10.0	
Rwanda	1,374	1.0	
Burundi	1,131	1.1	
Sierra Leone	909	1.2	
Congo-Kinshasa	764	2.8	
Tanzania	764	2.8	
Uganda	639	3.7	
Mali	624	3.0	
Madagascar	557	4.1	
Niger	548	1.5	
Zambia	545	7.1	
Mauritania	473	2.3	
Cameroun	465	9.5	
Burkina Faso	456	1.3	
Guinea	449	3.2	
CAR	439	0.9	
Liberia	414	2.1	

Congo-Brazzaville	406	5.2
Cote d' Ivoire	400	19.7
Ghana	397	6.2
Chad	359	1.0
Benin	324	1.5
Togo	298	1.5
Angola	260	10.6
Equatorial Guinea	249	0.3
Kenya	238	6.8
Senegal	231	3.6

The implication of this gross economic bondage is that African governments are now stooges at the hand of donor agencies and imperialist government, doing their biding thus becoming instruments at their hand for furtherance of neocolonialism through the application of doubtful and dubious economic policies that encourage the pauperization of Africa women and children in particular and African humanity in general. Worthy of mention among these economic policies of doubtful value is the Structural Adjustment Programme which has not recorded any success in almost all the countries that adopted it. Rather it has increased poverty; misery and squalor of which the most affected are women and children.

According to J.I Lugalla in his report titled, impact of SAP on women and children Health in Tanzania: "on 5th of September 1988, the daily newspaper of the Tanzania government, reported that during the first thirteen weeks of the year, 71 mothers died during labour in the Mumbele medical center, this number was four times the death rate of previous year. This increase appeared to be due to shortage of blood and essential obstetric drug such as lasix, diazepam erometrime, pitoci and hydrolyzing. The shortage of blood was attributed to a lack of transport from donor to recipients.

"In Tanzania, SAPs are negatively affecting the health of women and children in various ways. The rising cost of living increased production cost in the rural agricultural economy where most of the resources are generated by women and stiff competition with minimal returns in the urban informal sector have increase women's responsibility in the domestic household economy. The work load of women had increase with concomitant increasing rates of pauperization, poverty and misery. The women's working day is much long than the men's. An average woman work more than 16 hours per day, they wake up at 4.30 or 5.00am in many places and do not rest until 9.30pm or later. Data production by the Danish international Development Agency (DANIDA) in four villages of this Region, show that 25 percent of women's working hours (totaling 14 hours) was devoted to farm work, 28 percent to food preparation, 8 percent to other activities and only 14 percent to child care, 15 percent to other activities and only 14 percent to resting. Women have remained responsible for domestic work and maintaining their household while expansion in school enrolment has increased their work load as access to the labour of older children becomes seasonal. However, due to SAP, children in some families are dropping out of school in order to assist in the household domestic economy in petty trading activities.

"Erosion of real income and increasing poverty has intensified gender inequality and the power of men over women in almost all sphere of social life. This has increased gender exploitation since the majority of women particularly in urban areas depend on their husband's incomes. Even in situations, where women earn the money at the day it is the husbands who normally determine how the money is to be used. Since women are the mainstay of the household economy, decision unfavourable to them has become detrimental to the population as a whole. This situation is with deleterious effects to their health. The majority of urban women are being forced to secure their means of livelihood via marginal informal economic activities which lack safety and job security. Others have joined the entertainment industry where they have multiple sex partners in order to ensure their own and family survival. To some women, commercial sex has become necessary for them to support themselves and their dependants. The presence of the deadly HIV virus has turned prostitution from a survival strategy into a death strategy, on the other hand, erosion of women's income earning power particularly those who are married, means increasing household poverty thereby eroding the opportunities women currently have.To determine the mode of their emotional and sexual relations with their husbands for them to support themselves and their dependents due to poverty, women are forced to maintain marriage relations, not only because they fear the negative stigma of divorce inherent in Tanzania society, but because under such circumstances marriage becomes a survival strategy. The use of condoms in such relations becomes a taboo, sexual pleasure become meaningless and such women continue to remain objects of men's sexual pleasure and drives. This is reflected in the following comment of the married women, in Dare salaam: "We women have problem. We nowadays depend much on our husbands because life is difficult, even if your husband is promiscuous, you have to tolerate. If you desert him, where will you go? How are you going to survive? Who else will marry somebody with children already? Anyway, you have to tolerate. I am sure some women get HIV/AIDS in their own bedroom". It is now evident in Tanzania and most African countries that SAP has done and continues to do more harm than good to the general population. As far as health sector is concerned, the basic right to good health has been curtailed, women and children are suffering most as a result. By affecting women negatively, SAP are basically threatening the whole system of human reproduction in

Tanzania. The role of women as dual producers and reproducers, yet in Tanzania they are producing by sheer luck. At the same time, due to difficult conditions of life in rural areas, men are migrating to urban areas in search of waged employment, mostly without their families. Hence women who remain in the rural areas suffer from increased poverty, lack of companionship and risk HIV infection from HIV-positive returning husband.

From these expressions, we have seen in detailed explanation what Structural Adjustment programme, a dubious economic policy imported by men who are willing tools at the hands of the empirical community, the donor countries and their agencies have done to Africa. We have seen the continuous institutionalization of misery, squalor and death of the masses particularly women and children. We have observed with shock the deep rooted chain of mess resulting from the evil chain of loan and aids under tasking, demanding and dubious conditions – the squandering and looting of such loan and aid back into private accounts in the imperial nations –the final victim helpless women and children and other members of African humanity. What a circle of shame in the twenty first century.

TOURS OF AFRICA: A SUMMATION

We, after deep reflection came to the honest conclusion that there is a need for a change in idea and action concerning social and human development in Africa. It is women who should initiate and champion the change in consciousness and action. Africa bleeds from the deep wound inflicted on her by monumental level of corruption and visionless leadership.

Every country we went to earnestly yearn for liberation from deep sited corrupt leadership and unbridle tyranny. To our greatest dismay we observes that the poor masses particularly helpless rural women and children are bearing the burden in vain, as in its totality they have nothing to show for the questionable credits their countries acquired from developed countries, donor agencies and banks abroad. Governments and politicians across the continent acquired huge capital as repayable credit from the capital markets and donor institution across the globe with the pretence of providing social services and amenities to the rural poor, pipe borne water, electricity, hospital, communication, schools and cottage industries only for them to divert the money into private pockets through a grand conspiracy with their foreign partners.

Please consider the account below: in Nigeria an organization known as good government project (GGP recently presented a sponsored write up in the daily champion newspaper on Monday Sept. 2, 2002 titled "US$ I.2 billion foreign debt. Mbadinuju,Nnamani speaks up".

In this presentation by the above named organization, they argued that the servicing of this huge debt acquired by the one-time Governor of Old Anambra State of Nigeria now split into three states namely: Enugu, Ebonyi and Anambra States have worsened their economic situation thus making it almost impossible for the state government to fulfill its obligation of paying the salaries of staff in the states civil services as well as the provision of social amenities. According to the write up, the states have over the years been saddled with the responsibilities of a crushing burden of servicing foreign indebtedness to the value of US$ 1.6 billion, which accumulated between 1979 and 1983 during the tenure of one time governor of the Old Anambra State-the precursor of the three states, such as: $13.039 million (N3.02billion) loan from Samuel Montago and Co Bank for fiber filament and carpet industry which was supposed to be at Ihiala, in the present Anambra state. The entire loan sum was completely drawn down, yet the project site was not cleared.

There are also the USD38 million loans, from the Royal Bank of Scotland for the Effium-Iboko-Onueke road in the present day Ebonyi state. As in the case of Ihiala carpet factory, the loan sum was drawn down while no work was undertaken on the road. Today, after over two decades, Ebonyi state is still saddled with paying back a loan that ended up in private accounts.

In like manner is the case of the 13.96 million loan of November, 1981 taken from William and Glyns Bank, purportedly for the construction of a Central Repair Workshop in Enugu. While the full value of the factory was drown down, it was certainly not for the purpose of constructing a Central Repair Workshop. Within the same category also are the cases of the USD 50 million from Johnson Mathew Bank for the Amaichi-Amodu-Agbani Road, the USD 50 million loans for the metallurgical industry at Ozubulu, and the USD 150 million borrowed in 1982 from Banco Exterior De Espana for unspecified hospital projects. The real tragedy is that not unlike the other cases cited earlier, the loan sum drawn while the respective projects for which these loans were obtained never took-off. In the case of the Amaichi-Amodu-Agbani Road the plantation project was fraudulently commissioned on video. But even more tragic perhaps is that in the face of the unparallelcapacity of the civilian government of the second republic in the old Anambra state which brought about the huge external debt burden, no official word has been heard from the trio of Anambra, Ebonyi and Enugu States that have borne the huge pangs occasioned by this unprecedented prebanotalism. What evident, is a conspiracy of silence on the part of the three state governments. A feeble attempt by the Anambra state House of Assembly in 2001 to unearth the finer details behind the staggering debt profiles was inexplicably abandoned.This illustration above is the lot of almost all the nations in Africa. However, it is glaring to note that in all these cases of governmental betrayal, no woman was involved! This alone is a clear bill justifying the clamour for a leadership in

Africa, propelled by women. Remarkably, the easiest path to corrupt enrichment in Africa is the acquisition of foreign credits with the pretest of executing some development projects.

CHAPTER THREE

THE NEED FOR AFRICAN WOMEN DEVELOPMENT BANK

MONDAY

A very large gathering of the members of the African Women empowerment at the village school field, listening with rapt attention to an address being presented by their leader who has just returned from an international conference on rural development, and poverty alleviation, which was held in Durban South Africa. The smooth oratory power of the women leader which was sustained by a very melodious tone, emphasized on the need for the rural women to determine their fate, and take their destiny by their hands, trough collective enterprise, sustained efforts to alleviate poverty, disease, ignorance and discrimination. "Where do we go from here? How can we solve these myriad of problems confronting us? Presently, our challenge ranges from cultural, social, legal, and economic to political dimensions. My experience in Durban has justified the believe that we cannot experience total freedom anchored on sustained respect of our fundamental human right, if we fail to take an affirmative action to reduce the scourging effect of poverty, disease, ignorance and discrimination, which in most cases are self inflicted, owing to our inability to build solidarity, network and consolidated advocacy". The tempo of the presentation rising to a crescendo, the speech almost becoming incomprehensible, owing to deep seated anger that is flowing from the speech by the women leader; her shouting rising to a pitch, consider the regrettable, degrading, appalling, pitiable, detestable situation in which we have placed ourselves by our seeming docility in rising to the challenges of fashioning out an acceptable method of solving our problem by ourselves. These methods will liberate us from the infamy of cultural and social oppression as well as religiously induced marginalization, but prompting our economic and political security as such protecting and preserving our human right at last".

A wonderful sermon to self determination that will enthrone and sustain social development, and prosperity among the women, and rural communities in general; Dr. Helen Ndubuisi, possesses an enviable charisma and instinctive zeal to lead, and effect positive change in the life of people. A commitment towards eradicating poverty in Africa made her to pursue rural development instead of law during her undergraduate days. According to her, committed pursuit of women economic empowerment is the only guarantee for the overall development of Africa on the long run. After her thesis at the University of Nigeria, she built the African Women Empowerment, foundation a non-governmental organization that seeks to champion the fundamental rights of women through social and economic empowerment, she equally engaged in other serious projects like the Ikeduru Women Community Bank, Umukabia Women Community Bank, Umukabia Women Skill Acquisition Center, Afuguri Women Counseling and Development Center through all these projects she has been involved in series of programmes aimed at enhancing the well being of the rural women. It is through the pensive commitment to the alleviation of poverty and suffering of women that has made her to come to the steer reality that economic enhancement of rural women and the reduction of poverty in Africa in general needs an autonomous, independent approach from the pretentious and unserious methods and procedure of governments in Africa, which are characterized by deceit, fraud, and inefficiency. This made her to undergo a serious research on the necessity for an autonomous financial system that will champion the cause of economic and social well being of rural African women; and as such had her doctorate dissertation on the topic: The need for an African Women Development Bank. Comprehensive chartering, unruly sound emanating from the crowd obviously in solidarity to the motivating speech of the women leader, the major line of discussion between her and the women is centered on liberating themselves from dogma, archaic cultural practices that have held them hostage, marginalized and socially degraded.

Helen Ndubuisi continued, "I want you to understand and realize that we have a potent force, a power which can be utilized to liberate ourselves from these cultural and socially induced inhibitions if we can maintain solidarity. I believe we can say no to wicked cultural practices like female genital mutilation, widowhood practices, denial of inheritance right, and our inability to acquire and own property. I challenge you all to take these efforts at building solidarity serious, for it is only in doing so, that we can say no to the continuation of these series of inhuman treatments meted to us.

The question is: Where do we go from here? How can we improve our economic and social well being? How can we ensure our equitable representation and participation in the governance and the administration of our community? Next week is the coming of age festival, I am sure all of us detest the barbaric infliction of pain, and at times death on our young daughters. Do you think this should continue? One of the eldest women in the village climbed grudgingly and slowly to the stage, held firmly by the support of a few women strives to call the crowd to order.

Mrs. Onyekwere continued thus, "women! I greet you all, women! I greet you all, during our days, no women can dream of challenging culturally established practices irrespective of its damaging effects to the physical and psychological wellbeing of an individual. We were made to believe that women have no right and we never agitated for the protection and preservation of our rights. Now, the order of things have changed, we are living in a world full of knowledge, and utilization of such knowledge in making human existence to have a meaning, therefore, we should say no to any practices or law that conflicts with our conscience" she withdraw herself calmly as the thunderous applause from the crowd over-shadowed her voice.

TUESDAY

Crutching firmly, a brown envelop which she has just received from a courier personnel. She was overwhelmed with joy knowing the source of the mail conspicuously written on envelop is Dr. Helen Ndubuisi, African Women Empowerment, foundationUmukabia Women Community Bank, Umuahia,Abia State, Nigeria. The addresser's address was placed on the top-left-side of envelop vividly stated, International finance for Women Development. On reaching her office, she wasted no time to open the mail as she sat down, and began to peruse the response from International finance for Women Development. The content of the letter was:

Dear Colleague,

Thank you immensely for your remarkable effort at improving the welfare of women. We received your proposal for financial assistance for the development of five women community base skill acquisition centers. Your programme, though laudable cannot be financed by us presently owing to certain considerations.

We receive numerous proposals demanding financial assistance, but we cannot attend to all of them, as a result of our lean financial position, and programme focus which is presently not concerned with the disbursement of micro credit to rural women in Africa.

We sincerely appreciate your effort, and wish you good luck in your future endeavours.

Sincerely yours,

Susan Jack,
Programme Director.

The foregoing is the intensity of the exclusion which women suffer in their social, political, economic, religious and cultural life in the African society. Contemporarily, this extreme case of marginalization need an extreme approach towards addressing it, thus the quest for the sustained and meaningful economic and development effort that would lead to an African rebirth.

What is really wrong with these international organizations? One will keep on trying to attract funding, to execute genuine programme and development project, but will find it difficult to win the sympathy, concern and commitments of development institutions and development agencies. Unfortunately, they will prefer to give assistance and aid to governments as repayable loan which in-fact will not serve the purpose they were made for and the poor masses will be the final victim of these development and policy crisis made by corrupt governments in Africa and international donor institutions". She rose up abruptly from her chair and began to pace thro and fro in her office, and she engaged herself in solitude, vociferation and complains. She obviously continued to ponder these seemingly endless exercises in rhetoric's till she was drawn back to consciousness by the knock on the door; entered into the office were the leaders of the women empowerment group, they include, the elderly women of the community Mrs. Onyekwere, assuredly the eldest in the midst, Ahudiya, Ijeoma, Uchechi, Amarachi, Ogechi, Mary. Dr. Helen made an immediate reversal from backing the door and stepped forward towards the entrance to the office. As she turned the knob, the door was ajar while the women flooded in, beaming with smile, she commenced a seemly endless string of careful pleasantries. "Women" you're welcome! Women" you're welcome! You will remain healthy! Women! May you live long! Women may you have the means to take care of your families!

Helen was wondering to herself the right topic to present first to the gathering. Among the contending issues to be discussed was agitation against cultural practices that debased the dignity of women, promotion of the economic status of women as well as the involvement of women in the decision making body and daily administration of the community. Intuitively, she elected to discuss first the burning issues at hand; women solidarity and advocacy against all cultural practices that constitute violence against women.

A systematic movement of young girls out from a bush path towards the market square, rhythmically responding to the tone of the music, gradually drawing deep signifying an end to the chorographic harmony and the community of ages between seventeen and twenty, all clad in the same type of wrapper, the popular Akwuete cloths among the rural natives, which covered only their hips and private regions.

Suddenly, the tune of the music which was closing in a lingual drawl came to a halt, also was the harmonious flinging of their breast, the rhythmic swinging of bottom of different shapes and stature was not left out. The beautiful beads that adored their ankle and wrist equally cease expression and so were the beautiful girls. All are now terrified; frenziedly calm like a cow waiting for its final end in a slaughter house!

The large crowd of relatives and well wishes are now anxious, waiting for the seemingly endless cry of pain to commence, followed by the sight of blood that herald the endless bleeding after the incision of the labia at the cervical region of the vagina of the young girls and at last, the commencement of cheers for terror and inhumanity! Helen was having a flash back of how she went through the terrible experience of genital mutilation. She was full of anger, particularly when she strive to ponder on the reason for the incision of the labia in the genital. Reduction sexual feelings in the female as such forestall promiscuity and enhance fidelity in marriage. She was obviously quarreling within herself, challenging the irrationality of such practice that she became ignorant that she was thinking aloud. She was prodded to reality by Mrs. Onyekwere. "Helen, we are waiting to hear from you, obviously we have many issues to deliberate upon, but you should present the issue in order of priority'. Helen recovering from the contemporary trance, pretends to smile, to subdue he anger, clinched her fist and proclaimed while standing. 'We are not going to allow that practice again, I mean genital mutilation, yes the young girls who have come of age need not to go through pain, anguish, terror and bestiality before they would be recognized as matured for marriage! Our role therefore is to agree that this year's coming of age festival is not going to be climaxed to a horrific scene of merriment, women do you agree with that? Yes! Every one Chorused simultaneously. As the collaborative uproar died down, Helen continued with her mobilizations. 'The community elders are meeting tomorrow at the village square; I want us to send a delegation to inform them of our decision'. Our decision would also be made known to all the women by this time tomorrow", interrupted Mrs. Onyekwere.

Mary, pronounced "Mmerii" by the natives signify her intention to contribute to the deliberation. She is known for her intelligence, tactfulness and composure, she is a hardworking woman whose hard work is justified by her flourished vegetable and palm oil business. "My major concern" she began, is to ensure that we build and sustain a very strong solidarity and extend this sense of solidarity to the entire clan, if all the neighboring communities embrace our zeal, ideas and belief, work with our pace and level of commitment definitely we would not only succeed, but our network would expand to far and wide and as a result ensure the liberation of womanhood' Helen and other women were nodding their heads in approval, but Mary was not done, she is yet to strike the gun

Now standing up to express the seriousness of what she is about saying, looked round the room in an effortless search for nothing, began with a line of questions, 'when shall women begin to own and inherit farm lands, plantations and other properties through their effort or at the death of the husband? We hear about micro-credit, which the government is giving to women in the urban area, we hear about free health programme, we hear about fertilizer and improved variety of seedlings for farming, when shall it be our turn to receive these? Development is far from us for no reason, do we fold our hands continuously? Can't we do something? In our last gathering, our leader made mention of a bank that would be responsible for the promotion of the economic status of women through the disbursement of micro-credit, training of women in different trades and developing the skill and capacity of women in numerous occupations, I think that is the only way we can conveniently secure our future and that of our children. We cannot speak out against all evil practices against us, we cannot resist the terrible pain which the society inflict upon us because we were first of all denied the means of survival by ensuring that no woman in this community is idle, it is only when we greatly reduce, if not eliminate, the present scourging effect of poverty that we can in solidarity resist further abuse of our rights, we can speak out without fear, for we can survive any reprisals from the society! She didn't wait for the wide applause instigated by enthusiastic clapping and hailing by the women to end, she concluded her speech, 'women I greet you all, may all of us live long to enjoy the fruit of our labour'."Agreed" Chorused every one of them loudly. The total state of deprivation, deep sited squalor that constitutes the lot of the daily existence of the women alongside affluence and opulence being displayed and lived by politicians and top government functionaries all the same is worrisome and confusing.

Ahudiya is a woman of a pitiable, poor background, born into a family of abject poverty and presently wallowing in penury. Presently a widow, after the death of her husband three years ago, she obviously detest a world in which she and her seven children live in a house of about five bysixmeter divided into two while about hundred meters afar is the house with generator which generates electricity at the residence of Chief GoodluckNdukwe, a brother to her husband.

It was a terrible difference between the styles of life at NdudimNdukwe's compound and that of Chief GoodluckNdukwe. Whereas Goodluck lives in a well beautified and organized environment, Ndudim and members of his household lives in squalor, indecent and unsecured area; whereas Goodluck, his wife, their daughter Nkechi, Ijeoma knew nothing like hunger, deprivation and want, their neighbor was wallowing in deep deprivation, squalor and disease which later took his life. Whereas Goodluck has choice cars, which adorn the frontage of his palatial house during festivities in the village; His neighbor cannot dream of having one and had only experience the pleasure of a vehicle on few occasions he went to the hospital in town by boarding a taxi.

Summarily, GoodluckNdukwe, the brother of NdudimNdukwe of Okpualaa kindred in Umukabia Community, a permanent secretary in the Ministry of Finance in the State Civil Service represent the top echelon, the elite, you see one or two in various communities, they live extensively, and they have stupendous wealth at their disposal which far exceeds what they can earn as public servants. They have almost all the good things of life that money can afford, good and decent house in different exotic and reserved areas of different cities, both within the country and abroad, comfortable country home at the village, good drinking water at disposal, access to electricity backed by power generating set in case there is power failure, access to communication facilities, access to specialist hospitals, ability to send their children to the best schools both within the country and abroad, access to good, fresh air and rest. They look young and healthy; Ahudiya remembered vividly the day Goodluck drove to their house in his new elegant Toyota Land cruiser to see his brother. He normally visits home on festivities particularly during the end of the year. She very well recollected the discussion that transpired between them. 'Is there anyone in the house? Queried Goodluck as his vehicle pulled up in front of the mud house, 'I greet the people of this house he continued'. 'Ah Good-Good' 'Gov-Gov' holding his chest, Ndudim was interrupted by his ailment; he coughed for a while before he could continue with his pleasantries. 'Government man, you are welcome, when did you return? 'Oh I am just arriving; I haven't even got to my house. I got the information that you are sick'. Ahudiya came out from the back yard, dropping a bunch of fire wood, prostrated to greet her brother in-law 'De Goodluck, you are welcome', how is your family? I hope they are fine' 'yea they are well, my wife send her greetings to you, how are the children? They are fine' retorted Ahudiya.

Ahudiya hurriedly went into the hut and brought out two wooden chairs and made an effort to clean them of porridge stain. She drew close to both men under the huge umbrella tree at their frontage. Here are sits my husband' thank you' chorused both men.

As they sat down, Goodluck gave his brother an envelope containing a certain amount to assist him in paying his medical bill.

'Ah, thank you very much.' 'Do not mention, I hope that would assist you to settle your medical bill'. 'May God bless you, and may our ancestors protect you at your office, may those that hate progress not find you. Oh oooloolu or hu' the salutation was halted by the troubling cough whichNdudim has been battling with for close to eight years.

As the interaction between the two brothers was going on, the little beautiful bride in the front seat of the Toyota Land Cruiser was furious; she gazed at her wrist watch and looked toward their direction in annoyance obviously wondering what is holding her lover in such a dejected environment. As she strived to signal to Goodluck that he has wasted a lot of time, he only nodded his head and signals her to exercise a little patience. Despite his request to give him some time, the prodding by his love bird now become intensive, she is now totally worried, Goodluck, "Honey, let us go please, are you going to spend eternity there, I am almost tired, I am bored here, please come and take me out of this place!" 'Please Susan two more minutes, please let me round off, and bear with me, honey'.

Despite the rude interruption, the conversation continued any way. Goodluck, most of the development projects in the communities has stopped: our electricity project and the rural road rehabilitation has stopped, the contractors have even packed their equipments, the proposed health center has been over grown by bush, please what is responsible for all these?.

'E emem, you see, the government is in a tight corner, the government is owing a lot to banks within the country and abroad. we are using a lot of money to service these debts, then save the little that remain to run government, particularly the payment of salaries.' Not satisfied with the answer, Ndudim continued with his question, 'I heard that the government recently received financial aid from abroad for disbursement to our women, a micro-credit as well as the training old women on different vocations and crafts'. 'You are quite correct, in fact we have received a huge amount of repayable financial package from abroad, specifically the British Government for the alleviation of poverty in the rural areas. Originally, our intention was to commence disbursement of micro-credits to rural women after training them in different vocations. However, something occurred along the line forcing government to change its decision. Presently government is using the fund to develop and update infrastructural facilities at some selected government residential areas.' Ndudim was not happy with this answer, he asked, 'then what happens with us, the poor, the deprived, do we continue to live in squalor and disease?' 'Well right from the time of creation, there had always been the poor and the rich, all in the society cannot be well off, you must agree with me, there is no way government can solve the problem of poverty in our communities, this is the simple truth' said Goodluck. 'In other words, all the promises made by government about poverty alleviation through building of small scale industries and disbursement of micro-credit to our women are false', queried Ndudim. 'Well if you wish to take it so, e e m I have to be going'. As Goodluck stood up, Ahudiya come out to thank him for finding time to visit them. 'De Goodluck we appreciate your visit extend our greetings to your wife and your daughter.' 'Thank you very much, Ahudiya' responded. Ndudim saw him off and waved zealously as the exotic vehicle made a reverse and zoomed out of the compound.

Ahudiya still vividly remembers that remark made by Goodluck, a top government personnel 'there is no way the government can solve the problem of poverty in our communities'. This statement gave her concern, deep-seated worry whenever she remembers it.

As she rose up to speak the thought of that statement still worry her 'women I greet you all' Ahudiya's voice began to weaver, she failed in her effort to control herself, and she began to weep profusely.

Ahudiya! Why are you crying, what is wrong? Queried Helen, the rest of the women were equally embarrassed. To forestall the barrage of questions she abruptly bent down and wiped her face with her wrapper and rose to signify the regaining of control over her emotion. Having regained a steady voice she continued 'you all are living witness of how my husband suffered tuberculosis for several years, you saw how helpless we were, how difficult it was for us to go to the hospital and purchase the necessary drugs, he couldn't feed well, he suffered hunger and disease at the same time, he subsequently died, living me and seven children to daily fear and struggle to exist. I am afraid; help is not going to come from the government, before my husband's death in one occasion I heard his brother, Goodluck, telling him that government in fact is not sending in any credit facilities to the rural women, I look up to you our leader, is there no solution to this ravaging state of poverty?' Helen couldn't hold herself, she did not only nodded in approval she snapped "there is a solution, there is hope' I am putting up a revolutionary idea that will give hope and strength to all, no one would be poor or be deprived under the arrangement, for all would be empowered. It is an alternative to the present retrogressive, oppressive, corrupt and wicked system' I have a programme, both long term and short term all geared toward alleviating poverty among rural women.With time, I would unfold the plan'.

Helen looked round the room and noticed the indication of Ijeoma to contribute to the discussion. 'You want to say something IjeomaNwankwo, please let's hear you'. 'Mm mm women I greet you all' 'may you live long to enjoy the fruit of your womb' 'and you too', responded the women. 'I accept that we should mobilize ourselves to resist evil practices against women particularly genital mutilation but I believe that our agitation would have an impression if we have economic security. Women are almost the life wire of most homes particularly the widows, if we could be assisted financially, we would be independent economically and we would have complete strength for agitation without any fear. This is all I have to say, I thank you all'. Thank you' they all responded. Helen stood up; I want to summarize this deliberation. I want to remind you that…… she was interrupted by Onyekwere 'let us agree on the approach to be used in presenting our agitation to the community elders tomorrow, we have to pass information round the community this evening summoning all the women to the market square tonight, we have to ensure that we present our agitation to the village elders strongly, this is the only way we can succeed in banishing the culture of genital mutilation in this community, women I salute you all', 'thank you, they responded.

Helen continued her speech. 'Have we agreed that we are sending a strong delegation to the community elders tomorrow informing them that genital mutilation would not be practiced here again?'. 'Yes' responded the women. 'We have agreed that we would summon the women this evening to inform them of our decision, mobilizing all effectively for this agitation against female genital mutilation on our community; "yeeess" chorused the audience. 'As I have said on different occasions, these are our reasons against this barbaric custom.

'Firstly, female genital mutilation debases the rights and dignity of women, it is an act of brutality and violence against the women, it abuses and negates the fundamental rights of women.

'Secondly, female genital mutilation endangers the life of women, it is a health hazard, it leads to death, it spreads particularly blood induced diseases e.g. Human Immune Deficiency Virus, hepatitis. It equally leads to other complications which affect the genital organs and subsequently develop into serious health problems such as vestovirgina vestibular, cancer, menstrual pain, intensive bleeding, heart attack, poor sight, loss of memory, which are all incurred during the process of mutilation. There is prolonged administering of ashes, animal droppings and other contaminated substances to the open wound. This leads to immediate contraction of bacteria, viral and fungal infections and maternal deaths during child birth.

'Lastly, female genital mutilation is willful damage done to the psychology and spiritual state of an individual, like all acts done in ignorance, it is dangerous, destructive and hazardous'. As the entire women were nodding their heads in approval, Helen continued her speech; 'we are going to inform them that we are against all forms of violence against women, starting from female mutilation, finally the coming of age festival this year is expected to end on a happy note and joyful noise not the groaning of pain and the sight of blood, God forbid we detest that strongly. Women! Am I correct?' 'Y e e s, that is what we agreed!", they responded in unison.

WEDNESDAY

Helen was consumed with the challenges of enhancing the economic and social status of her community women. She was convinced that it is the only way their agitation will have a lasting impact. She had conducted series of investigations which had convinced her that the solution to the total state of deprivations, wants and suffering among rural women in communities depend on urgent attention that will ensure economic support to the women through disbursement of micro-credit, skill acquisition and training in different vocations.

She pressed the bell, tapped the knob of the door and turned, heralding the appearance of young girl Elizabeth, called 'Lizzy' by her boss; 'Lizzy please let me have three files on women empowerment'.

In this file were all the papers, correspondence and research findings on the need of women economic empowerment as well as strategies, she carefully placed the file on the table and waited to receive further instructions, 'please I am expecting Dr. OkonBassey from the University of Calabar, by 1 pm in the afternoon, I want you to rush to the town with the vehicle'.

Helen pushed a bunch of keys to Lizzy 'check the mail box please and come back immediately' alright madam, retorted Lizzy. She graciously left the office. Helen once, concentrated on her assignment.

'Alright I have seen it, I was going to ask for the paper you presented on the visit' remarked Dr. Okon. He readjusted himself and began to go through the contents of the speech which were as follows:

AFRICAN WOMEN EMPOWERMENT FOUNDATION

A CALL FOR THE ESTABLISHMENT OF AFRICAN WOMEN DEVELOPMENT BANK THROUGH THE CONVENING OF AFRICAN WOMEN DEVELOPMENT BANK SUMMIT: BEING A SPEECH PRESENTED TO A GOVERNOR OF A STATE IN NIGERIA ON THE OCCASION OF A VISIT OF THE AFRICAN WOMEN EMPOWERMENT ON 27-4-2010.

Your Excellency,

I would like to thank you for giving us the opportunity to address you this morning. Of utmost importance to the African Women Empowerment are the economic empowerment of women and the promotion of human and people's rights. We would like to deliberate extensively on the need of establishing an autonomous financial institution that will serve as a pragmatic catalyst in the sustained drive for economic empowerment of African women thus propelling a successful model in the struggle against poverty, squalor and misery in the new global order.

The major challenges to the African women human rights movement are still prevalent, surprisingly on an alarming dimension. Just to name a few – the rate of poverty and economic erosion, cultural and social discrimination, and domestic and social violence. At the height of these heinous crimes against humanity is economic disempowerment of women. Most women are living below poverty lines and as a result are falling preys to international trafficking for purpose of economic and sexual exploitation, while most become victims of slavery and under-paid labour.

During the special session of the United Nations Assembly tagged "women 2000 Gender Equality, Development and Peace for the 21ˢᵗ century" delegates agreed that although significant positive elements could be identified, barriers remained. They however, pledge to take further action to ensure the full and accelerated implementation of the Beijing platform at the local, national, regional as well as international levels.

At the summit attended by 178 member states mainly women, specific panels were devoted to many specific issues on gender equality, including good practices in gender mainstreaming, training of women, micro-credit programmes, protection of internally displaced women and girls, sexual and reproductive health, emergencies affecting women, gender perspective in various international activities as well as gender awareness. In its Assessment of the gains made and obstacles encountered in achieving objectives in 12 areas critical to women's achievement as identified in 1995 platform for action, the outcome of the final document were significantly positive. It noted that barriers however, remained to the full implementation of the goals and commitments made in Beijing. According to the document, while globalization had brought greater economic opportunities and autonomy to some women, it had marginalized others. While there had been increased participation of women in the labour market many women still work in rural areas and the informal economy as subsistence producers and in the service sector with low levels of income and job security. It noted that government had agreed to create and ensure equal access to social protection systems and provide safeguards against uncertainties and change in work conditions associated with globalization and strive to ensure that new flexible and emerging forms of work are adequately covered by social protection.

"To address the challenges of globalization, governments agreed to take effective measures, including enhanced and effective participation of developing countries, in the process of macro- economic decision making.

It was agreed that measures would be taken at the national and international levels to avoid any unilateral measure not in consonance with international law and the charter of the UN that impedes the full achievement of economic and social development by the population of affected countries and take measures to alleviate the negative impacts of economic sanctions on women and children"

The inability of African region to follow the momentum at the world level is an unfortunate threat to the sustainability of this movement in the new millennium. The sincere truth is that the task of liberating African women from poverty, diseases and sufferings needs commitment and urgent action quite different and autonomous from conventional development approach of governments and multinational agencies which are in most cases redundant, pretentious, unprogressive and characterized by corruption, deceit, mismanagement and backwardness.

Your Excellency, we hereby present to you the strategy for the realization of this goal.

She began to study seriously a recently completed paper which she titled: THE NEED FOR AN AFRICAN WOMEN DEVELOPMENT BANK. She intends to distribute the paper to all her colleagues, non-governmental organizations and institutions involved in women economic empowerment. The continuation of the message reads thus:

THE NEED FOR AN AFRICAN WOMEN DEVELOPMENT BANK

PREAMBLE

The world economy is experiencing a radical and in-depth change structure, marked by an ever-increasing globalization. This change bears new hope, throws daunting challenges and presents real dangers. One of the dangers for Africa is to be marginalized if it fails to become more competitive and if the prevailing poverty is not reduced. These challenges and dangers also concern development institutions, which must refocus their roles and state their visions within that challenging environment.

The conditions of the 80s and the problems of the 90s have brought into sharp focus the need to rethink and promote alternative forms, reforms and institutional arrangements and strategies for transformation of methodologies and provisions of social services and improvement of quality of life. The prevailing challenges encompass economic situations, governance and accountability of public institutions, and the emergence of realistic social policies and human development. In essence, practical, effective and feasible solutions are called for to extricate Africa from the current quagmire towards sustainable development. The task ahead is not just to change conditions and create new institutions, but to change consciousness in the process.

What is needed however, is realism tampered with inspiring vision for improving human development through a process of transformation and revitalization not only for existing institutions but also the system of value, attitudes and behaviour that sustain the process of change.

Africa needs a radical and visionary approach that will enhance the quality of life of more than half of its population – women, through a committed undertaking quite independent of African governments which often in their approach and methodologies are redundant, pretentious, retrogressively characterized of fraud, ineptitude and neglect. In this connection, there is the crucial need for total improvement of the quality of life of African women who have suffered immensely as a result of developmental crises, which incompetent leadership have plunged Africa into. Deep rooted corruption and irresponsibility among government and in some cases multi-national institutions has made the establishment of AWDB highly imperative.

Resounding the misfortune of Africa; the alarming food crisis, HIV/Aids scourge ravaging the continents, young generation, political instability and war in virtually all parts of the continent, low and dwindling per capital income, etc would not make news. But a positive idea so much promising to extricate the continent from the contemporary state of mess will make head line.

Considering the fact that the male dominated governments in Africa have wrought untold damage to the African humanity in the contemporary era of human history through the accumulation of questionable debt and under development there is the total need for a change in approach and practice towards development. There is the total need for a change in approach by banks abroad, development agencies and institutions, governments, NGO and individuals with interest in African development by assisting and financing the Africa Women Development Bank on-line, money must go to those who need it project. Let Africa Women Development Bank control one third of entire financial aid to Africa and you will see an immediate renaissance and economic growth. Take Nigeria for instance, the monumental level of corruption in the country has made the life of citizens miserable following the near collapse of virtually all social infrastructure including democratic institutions. An international news magazine, in its write up recently observed:

"Nigeria has received some $280 billion in oil revenues since the early 1970s through foolish investments, grafts and simple theft, this vast fortune has been wholly squandered. In

effect, because successive Nigeria governments borrowed billions against future oil revenues and wasted that money too, it is fair to say that Nigeria blew more than its entire oil wind fall. Nigerians are, on average, poorer today than they were in 1974. Despite the recent surge in the oil price, the country is saddled with debts of about $30 billion.Income per head in 1998 was a wretched $345 less than a third its volume at the height of the boom in 1980".

"Despite the pursuit of the various economic reforms and growth plans, economy watchers stress that growth has remained elusive for Nigeria, as the UN Human Development Index ranks Nigeria the 23rd poorest country in the world, despite efforts by successive governments at curbing rising poverty. The index shows that over 70 percent of Nigerians live in abject poverty. This figure, which was a mere 27.2 percent in 1980, leapt to 46.3 and 42 percent in 1985 and 1992. Harping on the extent of the scourge in Nigeria, Mr. Mark Tomlinson, the World Bank country representative for Nigeria, said 'about two-thirds of the country's 125 million people, in fact, 80 million people are critically poor". Almost nothing positive has happened in Nigeria in the past three decades". From the revelation above we can logically deduce that corrupt and irresponsible leadership of men has held Nigeria hostage for three decades, while the major victim are women and children. Money must go to those who need it, the economic empowerment of African women is imperative. Only African Women Development bank can guarantee this.

A bank totally committed to poverty alleviation through rural industrialization, sustenance of cooperatives and granting of micro-credit facilities to women. It will also encourage the economic empowerment of African women by assisting them financially in the acquisition of shares in blue-chip companies thereby ensuring they are actively involved in the economic-production sector of their countries, consequently promoting an equitable economic environment in the present global order. It is to be established in all the countries of Africa. For we in the tour of African team we have an idea, which we tagged "MONEY MUST GO TO THOSE WHO NEED IT CONCEPT"- THE AFRICAN WOMEN DEVELOPMENT BANK ON-LINE PROJECT.

This is an effort aimed at building a reliable development model that will ensure speedy, reliable and accountable disbursement of finance to those who need it; particularly rural women through an informative bank that will collate all the data of all the rural cooperatives, community banks and women based empowerment organizations in Africa. This will enhance their skill, education and speedy provision of capital. The money must go to those who need it concept should ensure that capital flow directly from donor agencies to the recipients without encumbrances.

In fact, it was in the remote villages of rural Africa that I was compelled to adhere to an intuitive summon to ginger Africa women to collectively advocate for what should be known as the MONEY MUST GO TO THOSE WHO NEED IT CONCEPT. It is this initiative drive that metamorphosed into the AFRICAN WOMEN DEVELOPMENT BANK ON-LINE. We were convinced that the only way to renaissance and sustainable development in Africa is by ensuring that money must go to those who need it. Women must not be docile any longer as available evidence has proved that a consolidated African integration and prosperity lies on them. They can actualize this through economic empowerment; this is the role AFRICAN WOMEN DEVELOPMENT BANK should play. Women are the engine room of African growth, they preserve the social values, promote domestic and industrial production. They are the majority; they are greatly excluded by men who have within the last forty years perpetuated the continuous domination and pillaging of Africa in collaboration with highly corrupt government, through greed, wickedness, bitterness and short sightedness. African women must rise to the challenge of extricating Africa from this chain of mess. The marginalized need efforts and commitment quite independent and autonomous. This is the last chance for Africa.

The quest towards the institutionalization of this pragmatic project is the prerogative of African women; they must through collective advocacy ensure its realization.

The bank (AWDB) will create a people oriented development strategy that will take much greater note of women by assisting them in the creation of goods and services and promotion of qualitative existence.

THE CONCEPT

The AWDB will ensure the speedy transformation of the standard of living of African women from that of misery and squalor to meaningful existence. It is expected to be an agent of change that will assist the totally marginalized women of Africa by assisting them committedly in the production of goods and services, provision of social infrastructures, empowering them politically, socially and finally, propelling qualitative livelihood among them.

PURPOSE

Our primary purpose is developing and establishing an autonomous, independent financial institution that will serve as a pragmatic catalyst in the sustained drive for economic development of African women, thus propelling a successful model in the struggle against poverty squalor and misery in the global order. African women should rise to the challenges of developing their cause themselves; work collectively to regain their fundamental rights; promote and preserve their political, economic and reproductive rights.

African women economic summit should aim at the economic empowerment of African women through the establishment of AWDB. The summit will galvanize ideas that will lead to the establishment of AWDB, and as well design a workable strategy for the smooth takeoff and sustainability of the establishment. We aspire to attract and handle at least 40% of all development capital and technical assistance that will come to Africa creditably for the speedy and sustainable development of the continent.

The African women economic summit will be a modest, carefully selected and well-articulated summit of at most one hundred participants drawn from recognized women NGOS in Africa, Europe and America, the academia, UN's representatives, the World Bank and IMF. It will serve as a primary catalyst for the articulation, projection of a comprehensive blue print for the establishment of the bank.

THE CHALLENGE

"There is no simple universal blue print for implementing this strategy (poverty reduction). Developing countries need to prepare their own mix of policies to reduce poverty, reflecting national priorities and local realities. Choices will depend on economic, socio-political structural and cultural context of individual countries, indeed, individual communities"- World Development Report 2000/2001.

"Nothing can be achieved without determined and enthusiastic effort by Africans themselves to bring about democratic and egalitarian development. More than anyone else, Africans know that the source of the future are to be found within themselves, that it is from among themselves that the people, the ideas, the achievements, the innovations and the great reform movements will come to lift their continent to the level of partnership in today's world".

"The path to be taken, the quality and quantity of the efforts to be made, forms part of Africans responsibility to them and to the rest of the world. No one can claim to possess a magic formula for successful development"-Federico Major, former UNESCO Director – General. "I believe the path to be taken should be directed by African women who are unpardonably marginalized, betrayed, shortchanged by greedy, irresponsible leadership dominated by men".

"Hopefully, this path to political, economic and cultural freedom would be a decisive effort that will bring about the total political, social and cultural renaissance of the continent".

"This path to be taken greatly involves economic empowerment of African women. The eradication of poverty which is the major cause and sustaining factor for all the abuses and sufferings we see around us. Lastly, it is very difficult to reconcile the current big corporation/transnational led process of a globalization with what it implies in terms of marginalization of developing countries, polarization of the world, even at countries level. What it implies in terms of inequalities, what it implies in terms of even conflicts and so on.

The fear of growing economic stagnation in the present global order could only be addressed by the responsibilities of African Women Development Bank and not the responsibility of corrupt governments".

PROCEDURE

The bank is expected to galvanize a responsible international financial system that will provide an adequate volume of external capital that does not warrant an unsustainable level of debt servicing. The bank is expected to attract direct foreign investment (cash inflow) from the western world without conditions, hinging upon the adoption of policies of doubtful value.

The bank is expected to work directly with stakeholders – the women in providing development and qualitative existence through the provision of micro- credits, training and manpower development.

African women should rise to the challenge of championing their cause themselves, they should work collectively to regain their fundamental rights, promote and preserve their economic, political and reproductive rights. African women economic summit should aim at economic empowerment of African women through the establishment of AWDB.

Groups tend to make escalating demands on the community, and these demands become increasingly difficult to meet. More seriously, modernization on an intensified level and on a world scale brings new social and material strains that may threaten the very growth and expansion on which modern society is founded. In this second phase of existence, modern societies find themselves faced with an array of new modern problems whose solution often seems beyond the competence of traditional nation-state. At present, the world remains dominated by a system of sovereign nation-states of unequal strength and conflicting interests, challenge and response are the essence of modern society. In considering its nature and development, what stand out initially at least are not so much the difficulties and dangers as the extraordinary success with which modern society has mastered the most profound and far reaching revolution in human history.

Your Excellency, being of the firm conviction that we are immensely qualified and prepared for the task, We of the Centre for General African studies with due humility present to you a proposal for the establishment of the African women development Bank. Also, we are humbly electing to co-operate with you persistently in whichever way you deem our assistance necessary for the actualization of this great task of economic empowerment of rural women. We pray that God will bless and sustain you as you commence this struggle towards saving Africa from the abyss of poverty, squalor and suffering.

We thank you immensely for your kindness and attention.

Sincerely Yours,

Helen N.
President,
African Women Empowerment.

Dr. Okon arranged the papers and carefully placed them right in the front of Helen. Well, Helen this is marvelous, you have taken this fight to different fronts, but honestly I am urging you to go the extra mile. 'Go the extra mile?' How do you mean? asked Helen, visibly surprised. "I don't need to ask you of the response of the Governments in Africa, so the choice is yours to go the extra mile and actualize it or to become a mere reference point in economic and social deliberations". Helen still looked puzzled 'I still ask to know the inport of the extra mile In this issue;" "Helen going the extra mile implies making use of every available legal means within your reach to actualize this project; Now sitting down ,with a low voice but with eyes wide open, obviously to make an emphasis ,you see, let me use 'we 'because I and our centre ,the Centre For General African studies are involved, this conference must be held , in fact our emphasis is going to be on networking with individuals and organizations of same interest. Contemporary global order is one being controlled by network of interests and I am well convinced that the only solution to the African problem is the networking and solidarity of people and individuals of common interest,in Africa, poverty alleviation and economic empowerment of the rural women. Helen continue to nod her head in acceptance and admiration. 'I am thinking of developing a networking pattern which I called Strategic Alliance for the Actualization of Africa Women Development Bank' suggested Helen.' that would be beautiful, I hope all the members of the alliance would be individuals, organizations and institutions that have burning zeal for the enhancement of the dignity and economic status of the deprived African women' remarked Dr. Okon. 'Of course, I will show you what I have done when we are back, meanwhile let's have a walk to the construction site of our proposed bank, the community bank project.' Dr. Okon was alive enthusiastically 'really, that's great, let us go right away.'

The Umukabia community primary school inhabits old patterned corrugated roof mud and brick houses sandwiching between grass, lawns and pathway. The sidelines of the pathways were adorned by big mango trees, palm trees and in rear cases wide bush.

There are beautiful, flourishing hedges of ixora and hibiscus flowers adorning the frontage of these remarkable colonial landmarks. It is one of these structures which are not presently in use that the leader of African Women Empowerment foundation found very useful for the establishment of the community bank.

This approach is remarkable, putting into place ideas long thought and held up in the consciousness as a child into concrete reality.In the siren and welcoming landscapes was where those landmark ideas were created, metamorphosed and blossomed, such spiritual and then physical relationship became a persuading reality that supports and encourage in the continuous quest to the beautiful, admirable end, the end of poverty, disease, ignorance and discrimination among women in Africa.

As they were walking through the path that led to the site of the proposed community bank, Dr. Okon cannot conceal his admiration for the serenity of the environment and effective coordination of the organization. Watching with rap admiration of the beautifully cut grass, the harmoniously positioned trees that created admirable shade and peace during the hot season. As they draw close to the site, work was going on with much intensity, the carpenter rehabilitating the roof, the mason, fortifying the walls while some of the doors including the entrance and the windows has been replaced.

Dr. Okon took his time to go round and intensely study the level of rehabilitation done, obviously satisfied with what he saw, acknowledged Helen, earnestly I admire your courage and vision, this is an impressive step l am of the firm conviction that the goal already exhibited will continue to endure particularly towards the proper activity, the training and disbursement of soft interest-free loan' he proclaimed 'In fact this is the last chance for Africa – this approach, like wild fire during the harmattan should spread to all parts until Africa is totally liberated" "This dream cannot die. Helen clutched a file of documents firmly with her right hand and placed the palm of her left hand to her cheek, she maintained a fixed gaze at Dr.Okonintensely.

The concept of poverty alleviation and economic empowerment of African women have possessed her so immensely that any statement concerning the development and enhancement of standard of living of rural African women instantaneously draw deep flow of enthusiasm and zest within her. The beautiful environments were kept lively by the sound from the carpenter's hammer, the masons trowel and harmonious tunes rendered by the birds.

Helen broke the silence 'l am even perturbed, l am full of fear, annoyed, I wish this project will be completed instantaneously. I wish the economic enhancement of African women will commence now and start achieving tremendous results now, as we are discussing here you can well accept the irrevocable fact that thousands of rural women in Africa are dying of hunger, preventable diseases, war ,injuries inflicted through cultural and social violence. In my fear, I have a deep regret that certain handicaps has made efforts not immediate, delay has become inevitable, this fear is an obsession I loathe so deeply'. Dr.Okon equally expressed deep concern that could be construed to mean fear, the fear that this quest for the liberation of the vulnerable poor in Africa earnestly need no further postponement, it should be immediate. In a very low tone but heralding deep conviction; He prophesied, 'well Henry Ford had a revolutionary idea about mass production of vehicles to reach numerous people at cheap cost, daring all odds he succeeded; Mitchell Gorberchev believed that USSR needs an ideological revolution, in fact the urge came at a time it is inconceivable that communism could give way to liberal capitalism in USSR. He committedly believed that the time has come for the liberation of his people from the shackles of one ideology to embracing a more promising one. Finally, in spite of biting odds, that intention has been realized, today, there is private ownership of the means of production and services in Russia, more people go to church and men can work freely in the streets with their bibles – freedom has come. There are other remarkable illustrations; one can go on and on. Napoleon Hill, an American thinker asserts 'that any idea which the mind can conceive and believe can be achieved'. 'The actualization of the dream of AWDB and the total economic enhancement of the poor rural African women whom the wickedness of corrupt leaders and ignorance of socially and culturally-induced men, abuse their right and also put into total suffering and anguish, is a dream which our minds collectively believe in, it must be actualized'. Dr. Okon continued. I can give numerous reasons why this project must be a reality; I mean the last option in the quest for a sustainable development in Africa'. Helen fumbled through the document and brought out a piece of paper, you can as well go through these points, they are my views as regards the necessity for an autonomous financial system that takes care of economic development and social enhancement of the poor African women. The expression indicates the following:

QUESTION

1. Do you agree that Africa's greatest problem, which includes war, debt problem, poverty, HIV/AIDS scourge are caused by corruption, inefficiency and greediness of African leaders?

2. Are you of the view that Africa is presently in a state of policy and development crisis?

3. Do you agree that there is a need for a committed adoption of new approach to development, which will give greater impetus to the initiative of the citizens particularly women?

4. What is your view concerning the establishment of AWDB?

5. Do you foresee the possibility of such a bank creating economic growth in the continent through practical effort of reducing the level of poverty among women and as such creating remarkable success as a model worthy of replication?
6. How can the proposed bank attract necessary financial support for effective commencement?

Dr.Okon was nodding his head in wild admiration when Helen suggested to him to turn to the back of the paper for the continuation of the write-up.

AFRCAN WOMEN DEVELOPMENT BANK must be a huge success. The reasons are:

(1) Owing to the total failure of government in Africa and international donor agencies in solving the deep-cited problems of poverty and suffering of people in Africa, there is now the compelling need for the trying of alternative development model devoid of corruption, inefficiency and lack of vision. This is the role which AWDB will play.

(2) It is true that Africa today is at grips with immense problems, but how can we fail to see, not only the downside but the enormous potentials of Africa, its reserve of enthusiasm, formidable creative dynamism that is only waiting for an opportunity to express itself .It is true that Africa in general is indebted to the developed world to the tune of well over three hundred billion dollarswhich was meant to be through application of economic policies of doubtful value, which are dubious in nature on one hand as well aspolitical instability, corruption and mismanagement on the other hand. There is yet an abundance of enthusiasm, faith and zeal which is necessary to prevent Africa from the brinks of collapse. Africans know that the sources of the future are to be found within themselves, that the ideas, the achievements, the innovation and great reform movement will come to lift their continent to the level of partnership in today's world. The path to be taken and the quality of effort to be made forms part of Africa's responsibility to the world.

The path to be taken presently to empower African women economically is through the establishment of AWDB. No one can today claim to possess a magic formula for a successful development model. According to James D. Wolfesson, President of the World Bank "There is no simple universal blue print for development, action must take place with strength, vigor and sense of purpose through the collaborative effort of African women, African government, multinational institutions and western world. This is a committed and spirited struggle that cannot fail because the economic empowerment of women will ensure the total empowerment of women and the full realization of women's rights. Below is a chart showing the approach of the concept.

- African women development bank on-line
- African independence monitoring group
- Rural women cooperatives, women community banks, women associations, etc.
- Individuals, farmers, traders, artisans, etc.

The African women development bank on-line will have a compendium of all the rural women associations, co-operatives and development organizations in the country, and deal with them through African independence monitoring group channeling finance, skill and information to them on continuous bases.

The African independence monitoring group will collect detail information concerning the need, level of resources, kind of training and skill needed by respective rural women groups and convey it to the data center for immediate response. Equally, it will have information on the level of progress made by the rural women through the use of credit and training made available to them. By recognizing the need of the women, the African Women Development Bank on-line will be in position to receive credit from governments and donor agencies for onward disbursement to the beneficiaries.

African women development bank on-line will ensure the display of all products of the rural women, particularly their crafts, textile and agricultural products for possible buyers within their country and abroad thereby promoting their economic empowerment and sustainable development of Africa through enhancement of productivity.

African women development bank on-line will strive to ensure uniform trade advocacy by women for a better trade relations with foreign partners contrary to what is presently obtained by the dictates of international trade conventions such as General Agreement on Trade and Tariff (GATT) and World Trade Organization, which are not favourable to Africa.

In the quest towards the realization of this project, the international body; governments, donor agencies and financial institutions should demonstrate absolute commitment in nurturing this new development approach as a replacement of this present system of inertia and frustration. Dr. Okon was through with the paper; she handed it over to Helen, held his hand skillfully to his pockets and began to gaze at the floor. 'Helen you have committed much energy, zeal and courage to this project, nothing is going to stop its actualization.' Helen urged him to go back to the office, they walked back to her office peacefully and full of inner peace, convinced that AWDB is the last chance for Africa.

The solitude ends abruptly as they were at the entrance of the office. 'Helen what are you going to do towards the immediate activation of activities at the community bank? What are the modalities and strategy to ensure that it is a success at the long run and what concrete plan, strategy and methodology do you have for the actualization of the dream of

African Women Development Bank?'.Helen offered an answer instantaneously, 'l will give you the detailed plan for the actualization of the bank through an African Women Summit, also I will talk on the strategy on the small scale which the method of acquisition and disbursement of small interest loan to rural women as well as the training and provision of productive assets to these women'. Helen open her drawer and brought out a file, on top of the file was the bold write up: Strategy for the Realization of AWDB, abbreviation for African women development bank which included both the very important questions from Dr. Okon and their answers.. She handed the file to Dr. Okon who flipped through the five page typed document with rapt attention. It began with the following heading.

THE NEED FOR AN AFRCIAN WOMEN DEVELOPMENT BANK

14ᵗʰ April, 2010

Dear Dr. Helen Ndubuisi,

Compliments of the season; ever since returning from the research trip that took us to different parts of the continent, I have been pondering on numerous significant issues concerning on the welfare, development and progress of African citizenry. The harsh realities that were the lot of rural Africans, poverty, disease and squalor were so traumatic; so embarrassing, so agonizing, so painful that it compels me to urgently reconsider this time with deep thought and reflection, your committed call for an independent autonomous financial institution that will champion with every commitment and zeal the economic empowerment of rural African women.

Contemporary economic principles, approaches and theories have come short of the expected results of extricating African from the imminent economic doldrums; there is an urgent need for a reform; Reform in approach and reform in consciousness. These approaches must be committed in involving private initiatives in the overall development of the society.

My very dear Helen, you could recall that of recent, many conferences have been held with the sole aim of creating a sustainable, consolidated harmony among men and women. The creation of harmony here involves equality, justice, understanding, respect, freedom, tolerance and fair play. Perhaps the quest for harmony is demonstrated by the view, that there is a resultant increase in social and human development by recognizing each other's fundamental rights.

Women liberation, women empowerment, women enhancement, women advancement etc. could not be made possible and university consolidated through the forces, pressure and collective resolve of women alone, rather the men in the civilized nations' display of the good attribute of harmony, would as a matter of social norm and civility accept the female, give them their due respect and regard in all areas of human enterprise. Perhaps the essence of the women movement in the contemporary period is the quest toward creating a world of peace devoid of oppression of any kind through religion, gender, colour, position etc. In this sense, women are inadvertently engaged in remolding the world, which had been damaged by the ignorance of men in their quest for domination, oppression, destruction etc. this is necessitated by the strong believe that people of the world should exist in harmony irrespective of sex or other oppressing factor.

However, this liberation from oppression is multi-dimensional in its application to different regions of the world e.g. the Native American would have a different priority in her expression of this liberation from the view of a native African. There is equally different opinion and demands as regards issues that should be addressed. The term oppression involved marginalization, injustice, relegation, violence which creates room for poverty, hunger and starvation, war and destruction, disease as well as ignorance, poor environment, poor standard of living, misery and frustration. However the rate and manner in which one is expressed or experienced in one region is different from that of another region. This is why it is of great importance that African women should have a formidable forum through which their peculiar plight could be evaluated and analyzed after due consideration and consultations. In other words, African women needs a comprehensive knowledge of what constitutes this oppression in the African region, what aids it, what can be done to reduce it from time to time.

For Instance, in defining what constitute oppression in the experience of the contemporary African women, one would discern a human being bedeviled with almost all sorts of problems that could be imagined-ranging from poverty to marginalization and from discrimination cum segregation to violence and destruct. Sincerely speaking, the major and significant social problem to be tackled is poverty which lead to other social problems. For any meaningful effort to be achieved in the quest of liberating women, the root cause of all women marginalization and discrimination i.e. poverty must be tackled and uprooted.

According to Canadian International Development Agency, "poverty reduction means a sustainable decrease in the number of the poor and extent of their deprivation". This requires that the root causes and sustaining factors of poverty be addressed.

Reducing poverty places a focus on people's capabilities to avoid or limit their deprivation. Key aspects of these are: recognizing and developing the potential of the poor, increasing their productive capacity; and reducing barriers limiting their participation in society. Poverty reduction must focus on improving the social, economic and environmental conditions of the poor and their access to decision making. "Poverty-reduction activities should be carried out in a manner which provides sustainability, builds self-reliance, and avoids dependency relationships among donors, partners and beneficiaries".Also in the forward to the publication, World Human Development Report; the President of the World Bank James D. Wolferson observed "poverty amid plenty is the World's greatest challenge. We at the Bank have made it our mission to fight poverty with passion and professionalism, putting it as the center of all the work we do. And we have recognized that successful development requires a comprehensive; multifaceted and properly integrated mandate."

KabiruKinyanyui, writing on African perspectives observed that "the conditions of the eighties and the onset of the nineties have brought into sharp focus the need to rethink and promote alternative forms, reforms and institutional arrangements and strategies for the transforming of methodologies of provision of education and improvement of quality. The prevailing challenges encompass economic situations, governance and accountability of public institutions, the emergence of realistic social policies for human development. In essence, practical, effective and feasible solutions are called for to extricate Africa from the current quagmire towards sustainable development. The task ahead is "not just to change conditions and create new institutions, but to change consciousness in the process". Is this a utopian ideal or something which is in the realm of possibilities? What is needed, however, is realistic…… tempered with some inspiring vision for improving human development through a process of transformation and revitalization not only of existing institutions, but also the system of values, attitudes and behaviour that sustain the process of change". There is an urgent need for this change in orientation, consciousness and value system.

According to the World Bank, World Development Report for 2000 AD, "poor people live without Fundamental freedoms of action and choice that the better-off take for granted. They often lack adequate food and shelter, education and health, deprivations that keep them from leading the kind of life that everyone values. They also face extreme vulnerability to ill health, economic dislocation and natural disasters, and they are often exposed to ill treatment by institutions of the state and society and are powerless to influence key decisions affecting their lives. These are all dimensions of poverty".

For example, poor people frequently do not receive the benefits of public investment in education and health, and they are often the victims of corruption and arbitrariness on the part of the state. Poverty outcomes are also greatly affected by social norms, values and customary practices that within the family, community, or the market lead to exclusion of women, ethnic and racial groups or the socially disadvantaged. This is why facilitating the empowerment of poor people-by making state and social institutions more responsive to them is also a key to reducing poverty. Vulnerability to external and largely uncontrollable events –illness, violence, economic shocks, bad weather, natural disasters-reinforce poor people's sense of ill being, exacerbates their material poverty, and weakens their bargaining position. This is why enhancing security-by reducing the risk of such event as wars, disease, economics crises, and natural disasters – is a key to reducing poverty and so is reducing poor people's vulnerability to risks and putting in place mechanism to help them cope with adverse shocks"

"The World has deep poverty amid plenty, of the world's 6 billion people, 2.8billion- almost half, live on less than $2 a day and 1.2billion-a fifth –live on less than $1 a day, with 44 percent living in Africa. In rich countries no fewer than 1 child in 100 does not reach it 10th birthday, while in the poorest countries as many a fifth of children do not. And while rich – countries fewer than 5 percent of all children under five are malnourished in poor countries as many as 50 percent are. This destitution persists even though human conditions have improved more in the past century than in the rest of history-global wealth, global connections and technological capacities have never been greater. But the destitution of these global gains is extraordinarily unequal. People live on less than $1 a day, the average in the poorest 20 countries- a gap that has doubled in the past 40 years. The experience in different parts of the world has been very diverse.

My dear Helen, from the issues raised above, you can agree, poverty is more significant and compelling in rural Africa and affects mostly women. What is it we didn't see! What is it we do not hear? We are confronted by numerous social problems – little boys and girls going to bed hungry, women resorting to prostitution owing to harsh economic realities, little children dying as a result of poor nutrition and no medical attention.

My dear Helen, do we not realize the wickedness and care free attitudes of governments in Africa? They obtain loan and abandon the projects for which they obtain the loan. They resort to debt servicing with the little finance left with the government for the overall development of the nation. They destroy all that is left of the moral values of the society through greed; accusations and suspicion, promote ethnic clashes, hatred, animosity, strife, confusion and war. They maim, rape, kill innocent children and women, they loot and milk the country dry!,through the pillaging, bunkering, exploiting and misappropriation of the natural wealth and the treasury of their country there-by maximizing misery; what a shame?

Sincerely speaking, I believe in your project, I believe that African women can only be liberated through Economic empowerment, like women all over world. The challenge of the new millennium should be a concerned war against inequality and other forms of human induced disequilibria that bring about poverty. The problem of insecurity; man is no longer secured on earth owing to wide scale environmental problems, which include poverty, disease, violence and ignorance. Amidst this state of insecurity is the existence of numerous national governments and multi-national organizations that are continuously in search through committed action, at times to provide adequate security and the total eradication of poverty, disease, violence and ignorance. In spite of the sincere and committed effort of the multinational bodies and numerous national government, however, poverty, disease, violence and ignorance is pervading at a frightening dimension.

Numerous people particularly in Africa die of hunger daily, people die albeit miserably under terror and violence on daily bases in numerous zones of the globe as a result of war and internal violence. The health situation had gone bad, to the extent that numerous diseases once thought to have been captured and eradicated by the wonders of science are now back, resistant to drugs and killing people in frightening proportions. Our cities and villages are now polluted by noise, poisonous gases and threatened by mining and other activities by man. While about a half of our population are homeless and countless others living in appalling and squalid environment, while discrimination against women continues unabated. These numerous problems give every person cause to worry, particularly at this age of scientific and technological breakthrough and advancement in the socialization of man. The significant question that borders humanity are:

1. *In the midst of great progress in technological, scientific knowledge and the socialization of humanity why is misery and suffering increasing on an alarming dimension?*
2. *In the midst of numerous programme and efforts of governments, multinational institutions and NGOs why is poverty, disease, hunger, violence, ignorance and general insecurity threatening the mere existence of humanity?*
3. *What has been responsible for the inability of humanity in eradicating poverty, disease, violence and ignorance?*
4. *What is the solution to these problems that confront humanity?*
5. *Why is marginalization against women so glaring and manifesting itself significantly in Africa?*
6. *What can be done urgently to stop the pitiable and detestable economic marginalization and cultural oppression which women in Africa suffer?*

In sincere and committed quest towards alleviating the rampaging state of insecurity, particularly the abysmal rate of poverty among women in Africa, the Center for General African Development and Studies, has to conduct an intensive research and documentation concerning the problem of insecurity and povertyalleviation in the new century. This will lead to a publication: THE CHALLENGES OF THE NEW MILLENNIUM: THE WAR

AGAINST POVERTY, DISEASE AND VIOLENCE IN AFRICA. The aims of the work are the following:

1. *To clearly define insecurity, persuasively with a view to compel governments to understand that insecurity in the world era do not arise as a result of military threats by other states or external frontiers but mostly internal problems of poverty, disease, violence and ignorance.*

   The United Nations Human Development Report (UNDP, 1994) put in the following terms. "For a long time, the concept of(human) security has been shaped by the potential for conflict between states, for too long, security has been equated with threats to a country's borders, for too long, nations have sought arms to project their security. For most people today, a feeling of insecurity arises more from worries about life than from the dread of a cataclysmic world event. These are job insecurity, income security, environmental security, security from crime these are emerging concerns of human security all over the world.

2. *To comprehensively assess the approach and action of multinational organizations and institutions in alleviating the scourge of insecurity, observing closely their role, achievements and failures as well as making most rational prescriptions for future attempts and action based on the experience and results ascertained.*

3. *To present a development model having comprehensively studied the attempts of various governments particularly those of the African countries.*

4. *The resultant publication, would seek to provide a most logical rational but persuasive approaches, methodologiesfor checkmating mismanagement, corruption and embezzlement; and promoting responsiveness, accountability, auditing as a veritable moral and social factors necessary for the protection of men and women against global insecurity; Particularly as abundant evident have proved that failure of governments and multinational organizations in eradicating the sundry state of insecurity in the globe is as a result of wide scale corruption, negligence, greed, financial inefficiency, poor sense of accountability in their approach.*

5. *To provide acceptable formula after critical assessment of numerous approaches that had failed particularly in Africa, ineffective control and eradication of insecurity in the twenty first century and in the context of Africa, THE AFRICAN WOMEN DEVELOPMENT BANK. The resultant formula which the publication would present*

would serve as a veritable guide for development planners in developing countries, multinational institutions – UNDP/WORLD BANK, IMF, WHO etc. as NGO's in their numerous activities. The resultant acceptable formula would:

A. *Provide a comprehensive formula acceptable to the problem of political instability and attendant economic recession in developing countries.*

B. *Provide a wholesome systematization that would checkmate incessant cases of corruption, negligence and unaccountability in the activities of national governments and multinational agencies.*

C. *Prove beyond reasonable doubt with concrete evidence that only a truly democratic society, were there is respect for the rule of law, high regard for fundamental human rights, accountability of public fund, private enterprising as well as proper and equitable allocation of resources would be able to secure its citizenry in the twenty first century.*

D. *Provide the necessary and acceptable principle that would guide the activities of governments, multinational, as well as NGO's in the twenty first century. This is to ensure that their programme are systematically and sincerely guided towards positive results as such forestalling any drift that would occur, owing to insincere conduct, unpopular ideology, theories and approach.*

E. *Champion the restoration, preservation and protection of the fundamental human rights of citizenry, particularly that of the women and the girl as a vital, inalienable factor in governance in the new millennium.*

F. *By the establishment of the objectives and policies the African Women Development Bank, it would present a vivid and logically sound argument with concrete evidence on measures to be adopted in the alleviation of poverty and insecurity. I believe I have said much in this letter, I earnestly hope that you are now strengthened, forthe project at hand; the establishment of African Women Development Bank is so great a project it cannot be toiled with. No amount of sacrifice made towards its realization is too great!*

Whenever you want to lose hope in the quest to its actualization remember that: all rural women in African living on less than a dollar a day are waiting for the actualization of this dream. All the children that cannot go to school, those of them that die because of poor nutrition and no medical attention, those women who cannot obtain loan from banks nor inherit property owing to cultural marginalization are eagerly hoping for the D-day when their tears would be wiped away forever by the vision and commitment of AFRICAN WOMEN DEVELOPMENT BANK.

Remember that our development tour that took us to numerous countries in Africa left us with deep realization of the penury and suffering which mothers and children in rural Africa face which unfortunately get worst each day through corruption and negligence by their respective governments. Hence the urgent and dear need for an autonomous economic and development model; a private initiative that would extricate women and children in African from eminent death and this is through the establishment of AFRICAN WOMEN DEVELOPMENT BANK.

I hope to hear from you soon as I am planning to visit you. I thank you immensely for your courage, passion, zeal and hope. The Almighty God will see us through.

Sincerely yours,

Okon Jacob.
Centre for General African Development Studies
Abuja, Nigeria.

N.B: Please give me a detailed description of the vision you have regarding African Women Development Bank, outlining the steps you intend to adopt towards its realization.

Helen carefully folded the letter from Dr. Okon into two and dropped it into the drawer.. She became deeply engaged in reflecting on the realities of the tour of the continent which they recently embarked on. In the tour of the continent she alongside other personnel of the Centre for General African Studies led by Dr. Okon visited virtually all the countries in Africa.

They interacted closely with the rural folks, they monitored development efforts of government, they faced the stack reality of depravity, marginalization, deep squalour which the rural African women and their children wallow in. They discovered that in most countries, the rural women live in different world from that of the government in the major cities, they in the rural areas knew nothing like good water, good roads, electricity or school and no health centre or rural clinic.

In response to the challenge of putting up lasting alternatives to the disappointing performance of governments across the continent she began to observe deeply her report of the tour.

Dear Dr. Okon Jacob,

In response to your letter, I am presenting to you detailed description of my vision of the AFRICAN WOMEN DEVELOPMENT BANK

Before that I want to remind you to note the vital need of dialectical materialism which admonishes us thus; to know the present we must look into the past and to know the future we must look into past and the present. Before outliving the vision and strategy of the project, may I quote extensively from the work of Abdul Rahaman Mohammed Babu in his postscript to the book 'How Europe under developed Africa' by Walter Rodney, "Are there shot cuts to economic development for the underdeveloped economies? This question has occupied the attention of many interested parties during the last decade. These include university lecturers, international economists, the united nation and its agencies, the O.A.U, planning agencies, economic ministers, etc. many international conferences under various sponsorship have been held during the decade and volumes of resolutions, guidelines, and learned documents have been published. The end result has been negative. The developing countries continue to remain under-development, only getting worse in relation to the developed countries.

By and large the question still remains whether we are going to repeat the same exercise all over again during the decade? From the look of it, it appears that we are already doing so, as the UN has launched the second Economic Decade with the same zeal and fanfare as they did with the first. The same appeal has gone out to the developed countries to be charitable and contribute 1% of their national income for helping the developing countries, as if this population of the world can continue to condone poverty so that the rich can be charitable. If past experience is anything to go by the seventies will experience the same disappointment which climaxed the end of the sixties.

What has gone wrong? Is it the very nature of under developed that makes development such a impossible task? Among the many prescriptions that have been offered – e.g. cultural, social, psychological, even economic none has produced any encouraging result. In fact nearly all of them have had negative result and made bad situations of the people, who have borne the whole burden of those experiments throughout the last decade?. This is the question to which all the developing countries especially those in Africa, must address themselves and the sooner the better because there is very little time left before our economies permanently distorted and probably too damaged for any meaningful reconstruction in the future.

"With very few exceptions it is sad to have admit that African is ill-served by the current conglomeration of what passes for leaders throughout the continent. While most of the

leader on the continent have no sense of urgency in solving the problems of people's misery-since they don't bear the brunt of their misery, the masses that wait.

AFRICAN WOMEN DEVELOPMENT BANK is a product of the conscience, consciousness and spirit of the African masses who have been betrayed by their own leaders; It is a revolutionary project aimed at bringing to an end the continuous exploitation, pillaging and exploration of African human and material resources by conscienceless few. This exploitation by greedy African and other foreign collaborators exacerbated ethnic tension and civil wars in most African countries. The major factors that sustain the bitter wars in Sierra Leone, Liberia, Congo Kinshasa and Angola are the bitter rivalry for the exploitation, misappropriation of national resources and wealth. Tension has arisen in most countries resulting to bitter civil wars leaving civilians numbering into millions mostly women and children killed, maimed, raped, dehumanized and abused.

Africa has the largest concentration of refuges owing to bitter civil wars going on in virtually all the regions of the continent. In all the conflict, the major factor that necessitated them used to be the grip of power and the resultant authoritative allocation of value i.e. national resources. Those that are raped, displaced, killed. Maimed and dehumanized are mostly women and children. The women are the majority members of the African humanity; they are not involved in any way in escalation of crises and wars that have been ravaging numerous parts of Africa They do not steal from the country and lodge same in foreign accounts thus, increasing poverty.For a meaningful integration to be achieved and sustained, for a meaningful development to be attained; it is this moral upright, honest and innocent humanity in Africa that should champion it. Apart from this, the circles of doom will continue.

African women should rise to the challenge of extricating Africa from this present state of inertia by championing and achieving economic empowerment without, poverty, disease, squalor and crises will continue.

AFRICAN WOMEN DEVELOPMENT BANK
THE LAST CHANCE FOR AFRICA

"Africa is failing farther behind the rest of the world in many areas of development inspite of growth in many countries helped reduce the global number of people living in less than one dollar a day or less by 8 percent between 1990 and 1998, the trend in sub-Saharan Africa is still in the other direction. The number people in extreme poverty rose from 242 million to 303 million, while the figure in East Asia and the pacific fell by 42 percent to 367 million. The international development goals adopted by the UN during 1990s and recently fused into the World Bank's targets, call the number of people living in extreme poverty to

be halved by 2015 and enroll all children in primary school. At present, current progress Africa will not meet the international development goals of halving the number of poor people by 2015, reducing infant and maternal mortally rates by three quarters and ensuring universal primary education"

The sad story of Africa seems endless; highest rate of AIDS cases, highest number of those living below poverty line, poorest in per capita income index, poorest in gross domestic product index, poorest in development growth African men shameless are at the center of this social and economic retrogression. Africans can no longer fold their hands and allow this circle of doom to continue. They must arise to the challenges of being a big economic player through economic empowerment. The African women development bank is the last chance for Africa.

The vision of the bank is to provide economic empowerment for the impoverished African women through training, skill acquisition and provision of credit facilities thereby equipping them for meaningful production, industrialization and sustainable economic growth. Already there is an outline of how this project could be actualized. This I will readout to you when you come. Thank you immensely for your support, strength and vision for African women through the establishment of AFRICAN WOMEN DEVELOPMENT BANK.

Sincerely yours,

Helen Ndubuisi.

P.S. I have already intimated some individuals and organizations about this project, soliciting their co-operation. This is a sample copy of the correspondence.

Dear Colleague,

RE: REQUEST FOR MEMBERSHIP: STRATEGY ALLIANCE FOR THE ACTUALIZATION OF AFRICAN WOMEN DEVELOPMENT BANK.

The African empowerment is an organization that works to promote the economic empowerment of the vulnerable group in the society particularly rural women; our activities include enlightenment. Skill acquisition training international networking and advocacy, micro-credit and rural co-operation; over the years, we have been involved in regional and international advocacy, networking and solidarity aimed at promoting the economic empowerment of African women. We in the Center For General African Development Studies have pensively completed a research work, a documentary and publication titled:

the challenged of the new millennium, the war against poverty, disease and ignorance. In the course of this work which took us to some countries in West African where we interacted closely with the rural poor, we earnestly understood that there is the need for liberation of the poor from the pretentious, back-ward and retrogressive approach of government and multinational agencies which are in most cases characterized by fraud and deceit. Hence the urgent need for independent financial institutions that would serve as catalyst for the economic liberation of the marginalized rural poor on Africa – THE AFRICAN WOMEN DEVELOPMENT BANK.

Towards achieving the objectives of the bank, we are organizing an international conference to be held in Nigeria on a date to be announced later. The theme of the conference shall be: THE NEED FOR AN AFRICAN WOMEN DEVELOPMENT BANK While the objectives: establishing a comprehensive method by which capital can flow for onward disbursement to the rural poor; coordinating, training and fine-tuning the operation of micro-credit institutions in Africa. Discussion and eventual agreement on the establishment of African women development bank stating the how, when and where with regards to the establishment of this bank will equally be addressed.

The present situation of Africa is that of poor economic and social performance and industrialized system which has further stratified and left the poor further marginalized. The situation keep getting worse every day, thus warranting a strong and committed effort towards addressing the drastic and disastrous consequence of poverty among the women in Africa. The major task being effective means of making capital accessible to the vulnerable poor.

Governments and conventional financial, as well as economic approaches have failed woefully. The present situation call for a private, autonomous initiative and approach striped of conventional, bureaucratic and unprogressive antecedents of governments in Africa. This makes the establishment of African women development bank imperative. We believe that this project needs proper alliance and networking of like minds, hence we are adopting you as a member of the Strategic Alliance for the Actualization of African Women Development Bank:

On the acceptance to be a member of the alliance, you are going to work together with us and other scholars, NGO executives, Business executives across the globe who have already accepted to be involved in this alliance.

The major task of the members of the alliance includes:

1) *Exchange of information and rationalization of strategy towards the successful hosting of the conference and establishment of African women development bank*
2) *Working in tandem with major donor and private investors toward the proper capitalization of the bank*

3) Monitoring the smooth take off of the bank on a drastic speed sustained by efficiency and good management toward making capital and training speedily available to the poor.

Please write to us urgently expressing your views and suggestions concerning the realization of the above objectives as well as giving us comprehensive information about your organization and others that would benefit from the effective networking which all of us shall build. While on receipt of your response we promise to provide more details on the conference. Thanks for your kind and urgent co-operation.

Regards,

Helen Ndubuisi.

AFRICAN WOMEN ECONOMIC SUMMIT

BACKGROUND

Poverty amidst plenty is the world's greatest challenge. At the start of the century, poverty remains a global problem of huge proportions. Of the world's 6 billion people, 2.8 billion live on less than 2 dollars a day and 1.2 billion on less than 1 dollar a day. Six out of every 100 infants die before their first birthday, of those who reach school age, 8 out of every 100 do not go to primary school. Private and public sectors must work together- along with civil society- both between and within countries"-James D.Worfersen, President, World Bank. Unfortunately, of the population of those living on less than 1 dollar a day,

Sub- Saharan Africa accounts for 24.3%.

Slogan: Let Africa women development bank manage 40% of all capital inflow to Africa and you will see the difference.

PROBLEM APPRECIATION

Women account for more than half of Africa's population. They participate in the development process in many ways, but their contribution to economic and social change continue to be inadequately recognized and undervalued, because our male dominated culture have given them an inferior position in the society, and custom, taboo, and the sexual division of labour keep them subordinate to men.

Throughout Africa, women's labour is vital to the production of goods and services. Now increasingly active in industry, women have been widely involved in agriculture, particularly in the crucial area of food production, providing over half the agriculture labour force in Africa, throughout Africa, rural women's activities in agro-forestry and soil conservation scheme not only provide major support to food production, but also add to environmental balance in the ecosystem.

In Africa, more and more women are entering the production and services sectors. Besides becoming prominent in formal economic activities as traders and home-base workers, majority of women in rural and urban areas of Africa, combine these economic pursuits with their vital social role as home managers and mothers, bringing up the young and caring for their families.

Women in Africa carry the double burden of poverty and discrimination; they are almost invariably paid less than men for the same work.

AFRICAN WOMEN ECONOMIC SUMMIT: IT'S NEED

"Some three hundred million Africans live on barely 65 US cents a day ofwhich about 60% are women. We can only see an end to poverty if private capital can come to Africa. There will not be enough public money to solve this issue" – IMF Director Horst Kohler.

If Africa is the most affected of the world's conspicuous social and economic inequality, African women yet are the worse –hit of this appalling state of affairs. Of recent, there has been much emphasis on the liberation of women of Africa from poverty, disease and squalor. Equally much emphasis has been exhibited by government and multinational institutions and donor agencies in incorporating gender issues to development efforts. Unfortunately; this does not go beyond rhetoric owing to lack of commitment, transparency and policy inconsistence by governments and in some cases, the donor agencies. There are abundant potentials to be tapped from the African woman, but this can only be through a responsible, pragmatic and honest private initiative of African women. Hence the urgent need for an African Women Development Bank.

Only recently, Mr. Mark D. Tomlinson of the world bank revealed."Nigeria earned about 300 billion dollars from the sale of oil in thirty years, out of this; more than 100 billion dollars or about 1/3 of this money was stolen. It is the kleptomania cabals that are responsible for this monumental thievery that are controlling state affairs in countries in Africa. Equally the donor agencies are culpable as a result of corruption and irresponsibility among its officers.

According to Graham Hancook in his book "Lord of poverty"-Mandarin publishers London 1991, most of the institutions concerned with development(the world bank and the various UN organs) never ask the poor how they perceived their need. The poor are voiceless in the project cycle or in the decision-making process... aid money hardly ever goes from the fund straight to the needy, instead it gets filtered in the deep pockets of hundreds of thousands of foreign experts and aid agency staff or else it is skimmed off by dishonest commission agents and stolen by corrupt minister and presidents and there is little left to go round". Except the burden of debt servicing which is then borne by the poor. Third world debts now are in excess of a trillion dollars.

"If we really believe in human rights, how can discrimination against women be tolerated? In practical sense, the cost to development of neglecting the unique talents of women are enormous. Morally, it seems to me admissibly , that at the dawn of the 21st century, limitation should be placed on women's fundamental freedom"…Federico Mayor, former UNESCO Director.

SUMMIT OBJECTIVES

The African women development bank conference aim at nurturing and sustaining an intellectual and development oriented conference that will instantaneously metamorphose into a developmental revolutionary process for the uplift of the life of all women and children in Africa, enhancing their livelihood on a sustained scale.

Towards this, the conference aims at assembling together development concerned experts from Africa, Europe and America and Asia for three days committed brain storming that will result to a lasting development network known as AFRICAN WOMEN DEVELOPMENT BANK.

This is a new and realistic socio-economic model capable of saving Africa. It will aspire to be the representative of Africa, thus possessing economic sovereignty as it concerns the continent; receiving financial and technical assistance as well as loans and grants for the development of the continent instead of irresponsible and dubious governments who retard the development process in the continent.

This summit aims at equipping the African woman to:

- Totally alleviate poverty in the new millennium.
- Restore and preserve their fundamental human rights.
- Fully develop themselves and live a decent life by limiting all forms of insecurity through a network: NETWORK ON THE RIGHTS OF AFRICAN WOMEN.

The new millennium must be a point in history, where mankind must utilize fully its potential to enhance his/her standard of living. We are committed to the total elimination of poverty, diseases, violence and discrimination.

In view of the above, the conference would aspire to build a network to be known as the NETWORK FOR THE RIGHTS OF AFRICAN WOMEN. Equally the conference would design a blue print and strategy for the successful take off of African Women Development Bank.

SUMMIT/CONFERENCE ARRANGEMENT

The conference would be organized in sessions and finally a committee will be constituted to comprehensively discuss, analyze and prepare a comprehensive blue print that will serve as a guide towards addressing the problems expressed concerning a particular issue. Thus there would be an economic empowerment session and a session on International networking and advocacy.

It is expected that committees would finally be formed to meticulously assess issues raised during sessions. Apart from the careful preparation of a guide of solving the problems raised in the sessional discussions, the committee on international networking and advocacy will prepare a comprehensive arrangement for proper take-off of African Women Development Bank.and African monitoring group.

SUMMIT /CONFERENCE PARTICIPANTS

Though the conference is mainly designed for African women, participants from other parts of the world, particularly Latin America, Asia and Eastern Europe are expected, while NGOs and institutions in Western Europe and North America are expected as monitors. Participants would be mainly people with high sense of commitment and leadership skills relevant to the actualization of the conference objectives.

SUMMIT/CONFERENCE FOCUS/SUBMISSIONS OF MATERIAL ON TOPICS

This conference is designed to achieve the basic objective of alleviating poverty in Africa, political and economic empowerment of women. Though we are still conducting research on these areas, selected participants are expected to present submission on the problems of poverty as it is affecting women in their country and suggesting means of solving them.

REGISTRATION

In view of the fact that we are anticipating a lot of applications, early registration is therefore reasonable. Intending participants are encouraged to submit letter of endorsement from their organization and/or network if their participation is on behalf of their group/network.

African Women Empowerment is desirous to ignite a dramatic, pragmatic workable approach that will promote the social empowerment of women on a sustained and consolidated pace. Towards achieving the above objectives we are presently working towards establishing a formidable network on the rights of African women, this involves bringing together all groups and institutions working on the empowerment of African women. The following are the steps we intend to adopt.

STEP 1: African women economic summit: the objective of this conference will be the elimination of all forms of violence and discrimination as well as ensuring the total restoration of the reproductive, political and economic rights of African women in the new millennium.

STEP2: The conference will design a blue-print/strategy for the successful takeoff of AWDB. The bank will be totally committed to poverty alleviation, through rural industrialization; it is to be established in all countries of Africa.

STEP 3:Introducing an economic project tagged INVESTING FOR COMPLETE CHANGE, which is going to be the nucleus capital asset of the AWDB. The bank through an aggressive investment drive aimed at creating empowerment, reducing poverty eliminating insecurity, creating wealth and good living among the rural people, particularly women and children will work through the committed association, the African Monitoring Group in embarking on a total economic development and sustenance of activities in line with the bank's objectives, particularly the generation of loans and credit facilities to rural people in small scale industrialization, establishment of relevant giant industries of which women will be major share holders.

STEP 4: Africa Monitoring Group: This would be supervisory, managerial, investigative arm of the network; it will ensure the successful implementation of the INVESTING FOR A COMPLETE CHANGE PROJECT. It would be involved in monitoring and scrutinizing of the activities of governments and multinational agencies in each country thereby ensuring that national and international policies and projects are meaningful to the immediate wellbeing of women and children.

This is necessary and vital for the effective usage of every available capital for the overall economic and social enhancement of the stake holders.

There are much capital and investment facilities in the hands of donor agencies, but the obstacle is the level of responsibility and transparency of recipients. Obviously, governments in Africa have failed us. They have nothing to show for all the credit facilities they have received from western world except huge debt profile, war, diseases and poverty.

In all sincerity, there is the need for a new approach in tackling poverty; poverty is the engine room that propels all manner of social vices, marginalization and backwardness.

The present situation calls for the adoption of a new approach, methodologies and practices that will not only lead to economic redistribution and growth but change in consciousness and orientation. There is an urgent need for a new engine for growth.

SUMMIT MANAGEMENT / ORGANISATION

The African women empowerment being an embodiment of recognized women movement and other institution working in this area will explain the opportunity provided through internal networking to articulate and package the conference in a most modest and organized manner.

The center for general African studies, research and documentation is a research institution that works committedly in areas of economic and political empowerment of women, protection of women from violence and brutality, protection of reproductive health of women, poverty alleviation; protection of women in crisis region as well as international networking and advocacy. The center in the cause of conducting a research that will lead to a publication and film directory titled, "THE CHALLENGES OF NEW MILLENNIUM- THE WAR AGAINST POVERTY,DISEASE,VIOLENCE AND DISCRIMINATION", understand that the quest for liberation of African women from poverty disease and suffering is a task that needs commitment and urgent action quite different and autonomous from the conventional development approaches of government which are in some cases redundant, deceitful, full of mismanagement and backwardness. African women should committedly build a formidable international network and advocacy that will champion the promotion of their rights through ensuring that government promises at international conventions and treaties regarding the rights of women are observed. Women should rise to the challenge of championing their cause themselves, they should work collectively to regain their fundamental human rights, promote and preserve their economic, political and reproductive rights.

PROCEDURE

1. The target capital asset of the bank for effective commencement would be one billion dollars.
2. All investors are invited to a study of a comprehensive report of our activities, which the monitoring group will place on website.

3. The major catalyst of sustaining and improving investment is the use of capital investment as a repayable loan to African women, who we have ample evidence to prove their ability to repay the loan promptly

4. Invest in direct production line and service in many countries, oil, solid minerals, telecommunication, transport, education, agriculture, banking and insurance.

5. Minimum of 100 dollars is expected from an investor, of this amount, 10 dollars would be used in investing for two rural African women, therefore for each 100 dollars; only 90 dollars will be consolidated investment of the investor.

STRATEGY

It is regrettable to note that in Africa, worthy ideas do not get the deserved attention, worthy projects are allowed to wither away by leaders and policy formulators who care little or nothing for the welfare of the masses. It is painful to know that huge fund go into ventures that do not survive generate or create services to the public. Corruption and embezzlement and lack of commitment have made the continent always seeking for funds which eventually are not channeled into areas of the greatest public good. We shall do all things possible to ensure the successful utilization of funds and record success either in industrialization or welfare services. This could be achieved through the following procedures.

- Affiliation with oversea bodies
- Creation of women development bank
- Refurbishment and resuscitation of our research and documentation center

By affiliation we mean a procedure by which our organization would co-opt with an organization that appreciates our purpose for technological transfer and exchange of ideas and policies for the total actualization and consolidation of our objectives. By the creation of a women development bank, we mean bringing into existence a bank that would be wholly and solely owned by African women for the realization of the purpose of the Center of Africa General Studies and African Women Empowerment.

The main targets of the bank would be:

- Assisting rural women in the opening and management of industries through the provision of credits, management and supervision.
- Establishing a monitoring group that would monitor activities of government and donor agencies from time to time.

- To organize rural women into co-operative activities and provide funds and managerial assistance to them.
- Encourage women to develop the culture of saving so as to generate fund for meaningful and collective investment (A financial committee is presently working on the blue print for the establishment of the bank).

By refurbishment and resuscitation of our research and documentation center, we imply a system that ensures continuity and consolidation of our manpower. We are experts in health management, economic analysis, policy formulation technological development and industrialization, agricultural and human development; our personnel need to be well-paid and retained on a permanent basis to position the center as a monitoring, supervisory and policy implementation force in the continent.

TARGET

Our major target is the alleviation of poverty and the consolidation on the success recorded as a result of this effort. Thus M. Khalid Shams- the deputy director of Gramen Bank of Bangladesh was right when he observed that"…poverty creates disequilibrium in the society and is the cause of much of the turbulence we see around us. Poverty deprives people of self dignity and destroys their creative capacity and is morally degrading, socially disruptive and economically wasteful, yet poverty is deeply entrenched in South Asia, Sub Saharan Africa and in the fast growing economies of South East Asia and China.

It is growing rapidly in the former socialist countries of east Europe and even in developed countries of the west, which have experienced chronic unemployment and gradual decline of their inner cities. Our national and municipal governments have generally failed to cooperate in dealing with the problems of poverty and the discontent arising there-from. In spite of the over four decades of development following the establishment of the UN system, massive project investment by multilateral and bilateral agencies, unparalleled development in technology and of course successive development plans undertaken by national governments themselves. Some concrete achievements have no doubt been made by the LDCS in terms of longer life expectancy, higher literacy level and rapid increases in per capital income, particularly in the Asian region. But the problem of poverty still remains quite intractable, and in some places, getting worse"

Thus poverty alleviation which forms part of our major target goes hand- in- hand with the successful actualization of education, food, health and housing for all, at affordable costs, as well as employment opportunities.

Perhaps the realization of these goals is as important as its sustainability; there should thus be the need for policy consistency to ensure continuity. In order to ensure this sustainability and continuity, we are of the position that the quest toward attaining this goal is two-fold;

- Direct human service investment of funds towards the uplifting of the weak and poor and
- Collective financial investment and credit service which is aimed at easy accessibility to credit, supervision, advisory and management assistance to the poor.

The truth is, in order to create this much needed continuity, there is the compelling need for the motivation of women through a comprehensive arrangement that will stimulate their interest in industry, agriculture and services, so as to create surplus food for themselves as well generate revenue through export.

In this regard, M. Khalid Shams observed thus: "There is however growing evidence that many non-governmental initiatives have attained considerable success in reaching the poor. In designing new delivery system we have to call through the evidence that is already available and decide on how best such system can be replicated on a large scale. Empirical evidence on ground suggests that the poorest of the poor and socially disadvantaged are capable of taking significant initiative when motivated as cataclysmic agent".

This can take various forms including:

- Organizing themselves and taking development decisions on their own
- Identifying specific development potential, based on the production skills that they already possess
- Initiating development through micro- enterprises, to provide easy access to credit
- Mobilize personal and group saving which can provide them with protection against numerous risks to which the poor are particularly vulnerable
- Empowering themselves through a participatory development process at the grass root level. They can bargain, negotiate and liaise with relevant government and government organizations to demand additional sources and services leading to a more sustainable development.

The Center for General African Studies and African Women Empowerment are mandated with continuous effort towards the social and economic enhancement of women in Africa. Though the final and authoritative document for the establishment of

Africa women development Bank is not yet out, as the final work of the financial committee would be submitted to the conference attendants for general review and endorsement, But major guiding principle that would be the work approach of the bank are those exhausted above.

The possible means of receiving funds for the establishment of the bank and other activities that serve as bedrock of the development process are:

1.   Direct negotiation with donor agencies for credit assistance
2.   Financial aid for government.
3.   Credit for individuals and organizations
4.   Direct investment from financial institution

However these could come as repayable loans or support depending on the negotiation that yielded the credits.

Though whether the fund reviewed is repayable or not the donor (government agency or cooperate bodies or individual) and recipients center for general

African studies and African women empowerment would collectively strive through good will and accountability to ensure the sustenance and continuity of development process which is main aim of the fund.

INPLEMENTATION OF SUMMIT /CONFERENCE RESOLUTIONS AND RESULTS

Commitments to international networking and advocacy will be the hallmark of achieving our objectives. African monitoring group will be properly positioned through proper supervision, auditing, accountability and high sense of honesty and sincerity of purpose. Equally governments, private institutions, donor agencies and international NGOs will be encouraged to assist us through collaborations, affiliations and partnership, so as to sustain our objectives, particularly, on poverty alleviation projects.

Also the conference in drafting the blue-print for the above projects, will be explicit to state organizational structure, management, activities, focus, funding, manpower, mandate of each establishment. The conference will be explicit in stating the when and what to be executed and also be responsible for its execution.

Once the blue-print for the establishment of AWDB and African Monitoring Group is prepared, we will strive to sell them to international women NGOs and institutions, governments and international agencies soliciting for their support and encourage them to be involved in the projects, since the projects are going to be managed as profitable ventures, it is expected that governments and countries will honor their pledges for the successful implementation of the conference resolution since governments, African union, African Economic Commission are expected to send participants. Thus the effectiveness of our international networking and advocacy lies in the understanding that agreement reached, are binding on all nations.

EXPECTED RESULTS

It is expected that comprehensive guide for the establishment of AWDB will be available (expressing-funding, capitalization, management, projects and focus).Also a comprehensive guide for the establishment of a pan African monitoring group for the total actualization of all objectives in all countries will be availableexplaining the organogram, manpower, activities and focus).

It is expected that:

1. In the first three years of operation, at least two million African women will be gainfully employed.
2. Small scale industries would be greatly encouraged thus alleviating poverty and insecurity.
3. At least two million African women will be direct stakeholders in production and service generating corporations.
4. Investors' dividend would double in the first two years of operation
5. The capital Asset of the bank will be more than doubled in the first two years of operation as assets would be invested in most of the operation and service delivery sectors of the economy.
6. This approach will be the fastest growing investment method.

Dr. Okon carefully arranged the documents as they ware and handed them over to Helen. Helen went across to the window and held the curtain together with a bind to enable air come in. The intensity of the heat is becoming unbearable, the situation is worsened by the non-availability of electricity in the village for close to a month now as a result of a breakdown of electric transformer which serves the entire community;Umukabia village and other neighbouring villages. She looked out through the window and saw a group of women approaching. The bell on her table rang in an effort to summon her secretary,' 'yess' answered Lizzy. She knocked and opened the door at once. 'Please Lizzy inform the women group to go straight to the classroom. I will be coming over there with Dr. Okon'. 'Yes madam' replied Lizzy. She immediately left the office and ran across to inform the women of the new development. Formerly they do meet with women leader at the training and development office which is just beside Dr.Helen's office.

The community open hall serves as classroom formed through adjustable demarcations made of plywood; it can comfortably occupy 200 people. It is in between the community school field and its farm with beautiful flower lawn at both sides.

The women comprising members from eight women groups, mainly from Umukabia village and a handful of leaders from neighbouring villages entered the hall and commenced immediate cleaning and arrangement of chairs, removing make shift adjustable demarcations to create a wider space for a convenient accommodation for the crowd.

As they settled down, knowing that Helen and Dr. Okon are quite close, Mrs. Ahudiya broke the news that it was not Helen, but rather Dr.Okon that is going to address them and possibly disburse the soft loan to them that evening. Every person became anxious and expectant.

The uproar died down as Helen began to address them. 'You are aware that our meeting with the village elders has been shifted till tomorrow evening, however, our demands would be made known to them with every seriousness and sense of solidarity, am suggesting that every married woman in Umukabia village should be at the market square by five, we should be there before the village elders. Our collective resolve is that female genital mutilation would not be practiced in this community again, starting with this year's coming of age festival, we are going there in solidarity to tell them that we would not welcome any form of violence against us any longer, all acts of violence against us-widowhood practices, early marriage, female trafficking, denial of political and economic rights and all forms of social discrimination will no longer be tolerated by us. After the deliberation with the village heads, we would assemble at this place on Friday morning, being an Nkwo market day to march round the villages and other neighboring villages chanting solidarity songs expressing our disapproval of violence and discrimination against women. Ovation in support of the speech became so loud, she later concluded 'women do we agree?' Yes chorus everyone in unison. As the ovation died down Helen commenced with the business of the day, 'well in our midst today is a committed friend and person who have given so much for the struggle for the enhancement of the rights of women, particularly economic empowerment. He will talk to you briefly.

Dr. Okon rose from his chair, women I greet you all' 'well you are my mothers, sisters, friends and even daughters as well, at least I have seen about three in your midst who are as young as my second daughter'. The humor heralded a wide laughter and cheers. I have brought good news to you; the good news is a sincere and honest approach in tackling poverty and promoting the standard of living of women in the rural areas. Your organization fortunately is registered under our center which serves as an umbrella body coordinating the activities of poverty among rural women. The name of our center is Center for General African Studies, based in Abuja, Nigeria. The name of the new approach is CHILD AND MOTHER DEVELOPMENT PROJECT; this project is borne out of the great necessity and urgency in addressing which addresses the plethora of problems facing mothers and their children in rural Africa daily. We witnessed the death and destruction of the young and old either by hunger, disease or bullets and explosives. The rate of excruciating pain which our people go through is appalling, alarming and frightening, we all strive and clamor for existence though already dead by the impact of the nauseating forces of disease, poverty, hunger, unhygienic conditions and miserable living caused by political instability, war and the resultant destruction of lives and property.

Africa, since the last five hundred years, had witnessed untold sufferings and hardship caused by both Africans and non-Africans. The agony of slavery was replaced by the humiliating experience of colonialism, brazen corrupt practices, gross negligence of duty, and total lack of will, vision and commitment towards transforming the lives of citizens by the post-independent African leaders.

In order to work relentlessly together towards addressing this system that has made us victims and casualties, Center for General African Studies, has come up with the idea of "child and mother development project". The objectives of this project is the total enhancement of the lives of children in Africa through concerted effort in improving the living standard of families, assistance to acquire education, medical treatment, provision of social services and amenities .Equally, to gear courageous efforts towards developing the potentials of rural dwellers engaged in agriculture, small-scale industry and other co-operative ventures; sustainability of rural development through sincere and honest utilization of funds courtesy of the utmost application of rationale and accountability. This implies continuity in development, organizational management and skills acquisition by rural women.

Thus the rural women would be the share holders of their rural industries where they produce the things they need most, determine the level of contribution they would make towards community development, conscientiously ensure the continuity of their industry through good business sense and patriotism, while the Center for General African Studies would provide required funds, technology, technical and managerial know- how.

This friendly partnership between the organization and rural women is expected to trigger off a huge success in agriculture-plantation, poultry, food processing, cash crops processing, food preservation and preparation, household utilities production, textile and clothe manufacturing, shoes and foot wear production, furniture, cosmetics and so on.

The Center of General African Studies aims at utilizing the good rapport between them and the rural African women to further educate them and provide medical assistance to them in areas of HIV/AIDS awareness, malaria, cholera, polio, meningitis, typhoid prevention as well as family planning by influencing government and donor agencies to ensure sound policy implementation and honest management of funds so as to witness good result.

CONCLUSION

Different positions are now particularly held concerning the activity of non-governmental organizations with regards to creation of goods and alleviation of poverty in the long run. Thus views that are in sympathy with the courageous activity of NGO calls for more funds to be allocated to them by governments and donor agencies so as to enable them diversify their development projects.

On the other hand, views and questions on the legality, morality and reliability of channeling huge fund to a group of individuals under the guide of NGOs, equally abound.

Perhaps the major weakness of the second class of people is their inability to be courageous enough in accepting the truth about the tremendous success of NGO in reaching the poor a statesman observed thus: "the non-governmental organization have a comparative advantage in delivering resources and service directly to poor people but they need to work together with the international and bilateral aid agencies and other important shareholders who have the resources but whose priorities are distorted in the plethora of physical infrastructural project funded by them in which poor people are often lost sight of.The time has come for a convergence of the effort of numerous parties and shareholders in promoting the main goal and vision of a word free from poverty.In line with the above believe the Central for General African Studies and African Women Empowerment basic principle of studying, monitoring and collaborating with the rural poor in providing them with credit facilities technology and skill acquisition and development in a continues sustainable partnership that would gear towards the total destruction of poverty, disease and ignorance, will continue to blossom.

This we believe we can do together with your kind assistance and co-operation in faith, perseverance, courage, discipline, honestly, hard work, vision and adventure.

I have no doubt made a long speech I will like to have your question in case there is doubt or confusion somewhere.

As women astonished by the uniqueness of the programme aimed at their total liberation from disease, squalor, deprivation everywhere remain calm. their question seemed to be, can this be achieved? Or is this another utopian ideology? Ugodiya and onyekwere simultaneously raised up their hands.

'I have a question sir', 'Okay tell us your name before your question' 'I am Mrs. UgodiyaOjimadu; my question is how can the proposed bank break age long cultural practices that do not allow women to own property? How can the bank empower women to participate in the policy making of their local communities and countries at large? I feel that real empowerment comes through development of skill and capacity of the individual to be productive creates goods and services and earn money as a result, is the bank going to sincerely make the task of developing the productive skills and capacity of the rural women? Thank you for giving me attention'. As Ugodiya was sitting down, Dr. Okon beckoned on the eldest woman (Onyekwere) to raise her question.

She managed to stand up supported by a fellow woman "May we live long, we pray that we shall live in good health to witness the realization of this great dream. Sir please are you assuring us that this bank will not be for the government, the rich and those living in urban cities, are we sure that those factors that led to the suffering of the rural folks will not continue, please who will manage the bank? We want to know if human wickedness will not manifest in its daily administration. How about greed, corruption and lying, cheating, neglect, war, conflict and wanton destruction of lives and property, if the bank can tackle these problems then nothing can stop it from achieving its objectives. I thank you immensely for giving me attention". As she sat down, Dr. Okon hastened to respond. "Well thank u very much, I can assure you l and your leader, Dr. Helen and the entire staff of our organization are working hard, putting in our best to achieve only the best for the African rural women. We realize your well –founded fears, we know that if good monitoring approach is not put in place, this project will fail. We are putting in place a sound monitoring mechanism to ensure the actualization and survival of this project.

May l present to you the comprehensive approach we shall implement to ensure the sustained survival of the bank and the lasting actualization of our dream in the long run.

Please Helen read out this programme to them in their native language".'Thank you sir" she resorted as she received the document boldly titled: African Monitoring Group and African women magazine, she began to read.

AFRICAN MONITORING GROUP AND AFRICAN WOMEN MAGAZINE

"In fervent recognition of your efforts and courage and in view of your avid commitment towards the enhancement and development of humanity, we wish to introduce to you, the AFRICAN MONITORING GROUP, AFRICAN WOMEN

MAGAZINE and MOBILE LIAISON OFFICE, which is the systematic procedure through which the MOTHER AND CHILD DEVELOPMENT PROJECT could be actualized. The reasons that call for the establishment of these projects are as follows:

To create and develop awareness about the nature of society presently and the policies and activities of government, donor countries and multilateral agencies as well as N GOs to ensure that the majority of citizens who are rural dwellers, though uneducated, but as proved by concrete evidence can read and write in their local dialect, are well informed through a thoroughly rehearsed, analyzed approach about the activities of government, international bodies and NGOs. Only an informed person can contribute to development, for example, UNDP is assisting rural women through its Women In Development Loan Scheme geared towards rural industrialization and poverty alleviation. But it is unfortunate that most of the rural women about 70% are ignorant of these loan packages. Therefore for a meaningful realization of loan, skill acquisition, and personal enhancement and so on, women should be informed, even in their own language.

Equally when UNICEF and WHO were carrying out their infant mortality project against infant diseases, the rural women could not capture the essence of the project and utilize it efficiently owing to ignorance. This is the case now in many African countries. Also a non- governmental body need not concentrate on government alone, but should strive to inform the rural majority and carry them along, this can only be done through an efficient information network.

AFRICA MONITORING GROUP

INTRODUCTION

In the modern method of state management, there have been of recent, a complex development which have been ushering gradual change from the traditional bureaucratic method of state absolutism and over centralization of affairs, to participatory, collective and decentralized arrangement of socio-political and economic management. Modern states are now embracing democracy.States are now eager to relate cordially with each other with the aim of fostering mutual help, ensuring peace, settling disputes and misunderstanding, promoting their cultures and welfare of their members. Of recent equally, terms like development, human rights, liberalism, open market, industrialization, women empowerment, and environmental protection and so on have come to dominate our consciousness. It has made a great impact in our thinking that all our activities in the contemporary world are weighed by its relevance positively or negatively to these terms.

No country can now boast of being self subsisting particularly the developing countries. States therefore depends on mutual cooperation and interaction, political and economic-wise with each other for its continuous sustainability and growth in the new world order. Thus establishment such as the World Bank, IMF, the African Economic Community, Arab League and so on are established for the promotion of mutual and collective assistance among states. States development outfits like British Overseas Development Association, the USAID, are equally established for the extension of this idea of cooperation and assistance.

States gain tremendously through good management, transparency, honesty, accountability and hard work. This is perhaps the reason for the successes being recorded in the Asian countries of recent in areas of economic growth. On the other hand, most states particularly in Africa are grossly indebted to International Financial Organizations, because financial assistance from international outfits and developed nations were grossly mismanaged through brazen fraud and embezzlement, corruption, ineptitude, negligence and dishonesty.

Honesty and accountability must be given a chance if Africa must make a headway .Equally, since men who dominate the policy making and execution posts of government in the continent have woefully failed this generation, is it not logical that the women should be given a chance, at least in policy initiation and management?

The need for the women to be given a chance is pronounced in the sense that they are the vulnerable group- the major sufferer of the wickedness and corruption practiced by men, who toy around with their destiny. When a loan or technical assistance is mismanaged, it frustrates development efforts and affects the citizens tremendously. Thus, it further aggravates the suffering of the masses particularly the vulnerable group;mothers and children.

African monitoring group will be a supervisory, managerial, investigative and execution arm of the network, it will ensure the successful actualization of the aims of African Women Network as well as monitoring and scrutinizing the activities of government and agencies in each country, thereby ensuring that national and international policies and projects are meaningful to the immediate well being of women and children

OBJECTIVES

The objectives of this organization are as follows:

- To embark on institutional-building and manpower development of women in Africa so as to equip and prepare them for formulation of policies and management of their respective countries.
- Motivate women to struggle for their due representation in high policy positions in their countries as well as international organizations, such as AU, ADB, ECOWAS, Commonwealth, and French Community and so on.
- To bring to the fore the brazen mismanagement and corruption that characterize the use of public (including foreign aids) in Africa and in that regard advocate for greater participation of women organizations in receiving and management of foreign aids in their respective countries.
- The monitoring, evaluating and analyzing the use of public fund either by direct government investment or donor assisted project with a view to creating an informed data and analysis that is unquestionable ,exact and dependable in the areas of fund usage and applicability
- To monitor, make a comprehensive, exact documentation and evaluation through constant monitoring of development in the area of health, rural development, population, environmental pollution, housing, education, manpower development, women enhancement, industrialization, communication, energy, portable water, mining, human rights and so on. Other socio-political areas including political participation, crisis resolution, policy formulation and execution, bureaucratic management and administrative reforms. With the sole aim of giving on-the-spot answer and information concerning the state wherever and whenever.
- To serve as data house, where information concerning state policy, development strategy and targets are analyzed and duly made known to not only the general public but the international agencies and donor countries. Thus, it should serve as an independent auditing body that would be giving honest and exact information that is freed of 'ethical and technical error'
- To bring to the general notice of the public through their publications (journal and magazine), the policy of government, particularly ,fund management so as to generate a well –informed populace and international community concerning development in every nation, so that proper step would be taken to forestall anarchy, dictatorship, violence and war, through the collective use of international political participation (democratic principle and practice) and international diplomacy and understanding. In line with this, accurate analysis and evaluation of events, policies, economic and political management of African countries would be our hallmark.
- To be established in all parts of Africa.
- To work conscientiously with donor countries, international bodies.

- To be involved in training, institutional –building of citizens of respective countries with the aim of creating awareness in political and economic life so as to avoid violence, war and anarchy
- To create an environment that will champion and maintain human rights, rule of law and as well monitor and bring to the general notice any attempt to violate human right and the tenets of rule of law in each country, particularly in war zones where children and women are major casualties.

TARGET

Our major target is to ensure that the vulnerable group (mothers, women, the aged and children) benefit tremendously from the assistance of donor agencies so as to ensure their meaningful progress and liberation from poverty and suffering.

We aim at being an initiator, implementer as well as an independent observer and supervisor of development activities in Africa. We aim to reinvent government in the sense of Ted Gobble: "obliterating the turf structure of bureaucratic governments and totally reorganizing around customers and their needs…" particularly at this period that there is greater call for the involvement of NGOs (female groups) in the management of funds for development activities. This call is very crucial considering the low performance of countries in the area of human and physical development with the attendant debt burden which are in some quarters tagged as 'bad debt'.

AFRICAN MONITORING GROUP: MISSION STATEMENT

Having realized that poverty and underdevelopment are the consequences of human folly, we wish to strive to infuse a new spirit that would defeat this folly.

COMPOSITION OF AFRICAN MONITORING GROUP

KEY 1: permanent secretariat, which coordinates all the activities of the sub bodies established in all countries, project them to international awareness as well as use their findings to determine accurate social and economic facts.

KEY 2: Secretaries established in each country, overseeing the activities as it relates to our goals in the country, receive information from the mobile liaison offices, analyze and forward same to the headquarters. It equally would establish its own monitoring mechanism to complement the efforts of the mobile liaison officers.

KEY3: These groups include voluntary members of the public who should include members of the academic community, journalists, professionals who would be detailed to specific areas to use their experience and training to supply us worthy information in that area, which we would equally incorporate into our publications.

KEY 4: This is made up of members of the mobile liaison office whose main work is to direct the rural dwellers, move from one place to the other in all nooks and crannies of the country and in the course of their development project, acquire worthy experience and report in turn to the country's secretariat.

KEY 5: This involves inspectors, who would be dispatched from time to time from the international headquarters to monitor development projects in the rural areas and report back.

AFRICAN WOMEN MAGAZINE

The magazine is expected to through a consistent effort, enlighten the people with the view of carrying them along in the awareness concerning sexually transmitted diseases, women political participation, decision and policy making, empowerment cum enhancement.

On the area of cooperatives, through incisively written articles, the rural women would learn much about organizing themselves into cooperatives; get directives on where and who to get loan assistance from both in their state and country; how this loan would be effectively managed, ensure honesty, accountability and social enhancement; acquire many skills in domestic and agro-industrial production; enlightenment concerning female education and rights; awareness concerning child abuse viz soldiering, early marriages, circumcision and child neglect; sound organizational skills and high sense of advocacy.

Originally, this kind of project(the African Monitoring Group and African Women Magazine) should be backed by a well coordinated communication network, this would involve sophisticated and computerized communication gadgets, many of which we cannot afford as of now due to financial constraint. But with strong determination, enthusiasm, courage and drive we would succeed.

Only an informed person can contribute to development. To this end, our mobile liaison office under the umbrella of the monitoring group would be involved in continuous interaction with the local, state and national government functionaries as well as rural natives concerning issues of mutual interests.

The major aim of these magazine (Africa women magazine) is to serve as veritable advocate for reform and committed integration of women into policy making and execution (economic and political empowerment as well as social enhancement) the magazine on commencement would seek to evolve means of gaining acceptability through standard and commendable publication, so as to attract promotion and adverts from individuals and companies. By these creating funds for establishment and sustenance of the project.

The magazine through life pictures depicting life in Africa would bring to the fore the living conditions of rural Africans and as such to arouse the consciousness of African governments to women as well as international community on the need for urgent social and economic reformation.

It equally should serve as a watch dog of both government and international agencies in Africa.

The magazine unit should in serving as information unit produce documentaries and journals all with the aim of challenging effort towards social reforms.

Co-operatives would be encouraged through the activities of the rural banks; the community banks would be engaged in the empowerment of rural women through skill acquisition and provision of micro credits.

MOBILE LIAISON OFFICE AND FUNCTIONS

The mobile liaison office by its nature, outlook, strategy and goal has three main purposes which determine its functions viz:

- Economic and social enhancement.
- Political empowerment.
- Good health and disease control.

For effective economic and social enhancement, the mobile liaison office should be much engaged in directing, redirecting, supervising, initiating and monitoring the activities of rural and poor women to ensure quick economic enhancement, social progress and sustainable development, these would be carried out through practical demonstration of small scale industry, management, agricultural cooperative, individual skills acquisition and enhancement, access to loan/credit lines and utilization, emphasis on participatory collectivism, accountability and effective supervision.

Equally, the office would be handy to explain in the most plain language new ideas, approaches relating to industrial development policy of government, NGOs role in the area of health, education, agriculture, shelter and human rights.

For effective political empowerment the office should aim at organizing women through publications and public lectures on the need for political participation in their respective countries, organize women in politics, and ensure that a proportionate number of women gain access to parliaments, government cabinet/executives and so on. Towards actualizing this, the mobile liaison group tacitly aspires, to maintain a committed interaction with rural women in all nooks and crannies of the continent, female journalists, civil right activists, students, female professionals and policy makers with a view at streamlining the march towards total and committed political empowerment so as to ensure that women know their rights, maintain high sense of advocacy and struggle when these rights are threatened.

To ensure good health, the office should engaged in mass dissemination of information on the control and prevention of diseases, monitoring of government policies as well as redirecting policies of government to ensure that it is effective as well as mass- oriented.

To this end, we are appealing to international women health coalition for permission to reproduce their publications on diseases and control in African languages as well as French and English, these publications include research analysis, essays in form of textbooks and tract. The two major areas concerned are:

- Reproductive tract infection
- Contraceptive

Our intention is to reproduce theses publications in large quantities and distribute them to medical and health workers, rural cooperatives, NGOs, government and policy makers, students and libraries so as to facilitate awareness and promote advocacy and government commitment to maternal health in Africa.

The publications affected are:

- Challenging the culture of science: Building alliances to eliminate and reproductive tract infections
- Reproductive tract infection: Global impact and priorities for women's reproductive health
- Reproductive tract infection in the third world: National and international policy implication
- The culture of science: REPRODUCTIVE TRACT infection among women in the third world
- Special challenges in third world women's health: Reproductive tract infections, cervical cancer and contraceptive safety
- Declaration of international symposium on contraceptive-Research and development for the year 2000 and beyond
- The contraceptive development process and quality of care in reproductive health services

MOBILE LIAISON OFFICE COMPOSITION AND FUNCTIONS

KEY 1: Women almost in all tribes of Africa are traditionally responsible for the sustenance of the family. This had exposed them to much toil and labour, particularly at this epoch of economic recession in most countries. In order to liberate women from poverty, they should acquire skills that would help them to create income through the generation of goods and services. This is the major purpose of Africa Women Development Bank.

The mobile liaison workers would train the rural women in the modern methods of making soap and cosmetics, building house, carpentry, baking, bead making and other vocations like tailoring, painting trading, food preservation welding establishment and management of small scale industries (bread industry, block industry, food preservation industry, fashion factory, footwear industry, etc.)

The mobile liaison workers would by their direct contact with the rural native in actualizing numerous poverty alleviation projects accumulate useful experience which would be forwarded to the headquarters.

Women should be encouraged through political education and enlightenment to participate in participatory politics so as to enable them acquires policy making and the execution position. The rural women and youth are the majority in all countries in Africa. They have the potential to change the social pattern with their electoral power.

On the economic front, women should gain credit to facilities without collateral or security rural women bank is what the mobile liaison office would manage to be established. Countries should appoint women into high policy positions with regards to economy e.g. financial ministry and state owned banks.

There should be incentives for rural women in the area of agriculture fertilizer agricequipments. The liaison office by direct mobilization of the rural women to achieve these set goals would equally report to the secretariat for onward lobbing of government and international organizations communicable disease and outbreak of epidemic

Equally they would educate them on AIDS/ HIV typhoid and malaria as well as sexually transmitted disease.Equally they would improvise means of ensuring that there is availability of good drinking water in the rural areas.

Children education and development should be given wholesome attention through direct contact with the child so as to develop his skills and mentality

To this end workshops and training would be organized for the rural child and the urban children to enable him/her gain knowledge concerning.

1.   Computer programming
2.   Good conduct and ethics

3.   Drug addiction and illicit sex

4.   Child soldering, violence and destruction

5.   Community development and skills acquisition

The mobile liaison office through its contact with the child would report to the secretariat for proper documentation and dissemination of information.

The mobile liaison office should ensure that there is efficient agricultural practice in each community with the aim of eliminating hunger as agriculture co-operatives should be encouraged. Plantation for cocoa, palm oil, coffee, sugarcane, rice, wheat, corn etc. would encourage good demonstration of irrigation crop preservation. Equally poultry and fishing would be given more attention as well as agricultural processing industries.

The mobile liaison office would create skills as well as credit to the rural area for production of food.

APPROACH OF THE MOBILE LIAISON OFFICE

The major approach of the liaison office is to demonstrate diverse development methods to the rural dwellers; monitor them to ensure they acquire the skills of management and accountability in order to ensure the sustainability of their projects

Another major approach of the office is the organization, indoctrination of women in political participation and awareness. The liaison office of this organization could have done all it can to mobilize women, support women in various parties to context and maintaining consistent advocacy to ensure that each party reserves a proportionate representation of fifty percent for women in their party nominations across the country.

Lastly the liaison office would be involved in investigating human rights positions, welfare programmes and level of involvement of women in policy making and execution in each country.

Only an informed person can contribute to development. Both the African Monitoring Group and African Women Magazine are working tirelessly to ensure the circulation of the maiden edition of the Women Magazine by November this year .The realization of this project depends on the financial and moral contribution of those who believe in the worthiness of these projects towards sustainable development in Africa.

Being aware of your remarkable zeal towards sustainable development and social enhancement of mothers and children, particularly those living below poverty line, we most appeal for your deeply appreciated assistance and that of your organization.

We look forward to informing you through the publication the comprehensive and up to date facts about development issues in rural Africa viz:

- Level of health and disease management
- Up to date information concerning the activities of UNICEF,WHO,IPPF, governments and donor agencies.
- Up to date information on state health facilities, management and so on in countries.
- Policies of government concerning health, women and development.
- Monitoring and evaluating the use of fund by women NGOs, government agencies, and donor agencies to ensure accountability thereby generating public awareness and commitment among governments, concerned agencies and individuals on the management of health and development in general,so as to ensure sincerity, courage commitment, vision and progress. Thereby raising of consciousness of rural women by guiding them towards social enhancement and political empowerment on one hand and informing the international community on the other hand thereby bringing about development, women empowerment and enhancement.

STRATEGY

The hallmark of our program is continuity and sustainability.In the spirit of continuity we should emphasis on the growth of economic project that are jointly owned by the organization and the rural natives in the area of production and services as this would enable us to cover more areas without running short of finance.

Committed zeal and courage should be put into the program such that no stone would be left unturned until poverty is completely wiped off.

The success of our programme in each locality will be skillfully introduced to the government and international organizations so that it would be applied in large and generalized scale.

Comprehensive evaluation and research would be emphasized to minimize failure while sustained effort would be encouraged for progress in all fronts.

SACRIFICE

If there is one thing all the majority of religions agree upon it is the concept of sacrifice. It is redeeming grace of humanity and connotes denial of self, the giving up of personal aspirations for union, association, fellowship common good and communion.

In its most noble form sacrifice is vicarious substitution it entails selfness at a mundane level it is sympathetic participation in the experience of other. It is an inescapable crucial and necessary underpinning of society upon which great nations are built, without sacrifice nothing worth living for can be built.

CONCLUSION

It is now well established that international organizations have mostly failed in Africa particularly in areas of poverty alleviation equally it is self evident that their failure resulted mostly from their inability to integrate the poor in economic and social programs that are being made in the continent.Numerous evidence abound which support the position that the poor if motivated and encouraged, socially and economically can are able to liberate themselves from poverty

It this great believe that builds this idea of pragmatic approach to alleviating poverty in Africa.

Any person who is aware of the tremendous achievement of the Carnegie co-operation International Women Coalition Centre for Women Global Leadership,The Ford Foundation Global Fund for women, The Bank of Bangladesh, Action International and other numerous organization in their respective areas of interest would not doubt the possibility of achieving a noble ideal no matter how enormous the task maybe provided honesty courage and vision is not compromised.By the exhibition of the spirit of philanthropy some flowers which might have blushed unseen are enabled to develop into full blossom?

It is one of these meeting room that Dr. Helen Ndubuisi, Dr. Okon and other members of the faculty in the Center of General African Studies Research and Documentation were brain storming on modalities for conducting successful and fruitful conference.

As the protocol officers made up of staff of the Nigerian ministry of women affairs and social development the conducting firm handing the conference, cyber network and staff of Centre of African Studies Research and Documentation were busy receiving conference participants from the airport to convey them to the conference venue, the International conference center, Abuja, Nigeria capital city all is set for the gala night which will feature a series of cultural display by cultural groups and artist from different part of the country.

The following day as well is full of fanfare and sober reflections which will result from land mark lectures and speeches on the need of power shift to African women.

At the bottom of the schedule is this notification of detailed analysis. Participants who intend to travel to special tourist attractions packaged by the organizer can stay for addition two days.

The second day of the conference is commencement of business in earnest. The major purpose for the conference is the actualization of African Women Development Bank for the economic empowerment of African women.

I wish to inform you that the session discussion for which we are here presently is to take off. I hereby call on the chairman of the session, Dr. Okon to present his speech thus declaring the sessions open.

The announcement by Dr. Helen, the conference moderator, heralded the commencement of session discussion which was motivated and inspired for positive results by insightful presentation by the lead discussant, Dr. Okon of the centre for General African studies. Dr.Okon elegantly and briskly moved to the stage for the presentation of this work which he titled.

WOMEN ECONOMIC EMPOWERMENT: A NECESSARY TOOL FOR REBIRTH

"The Nigerian population needs to be convinced that it is moral and fair for the international community to forget that of the more than USD 30billions that is Nigeria current debt profile the principal sum isless than USD 8 billion, over 20 USD billion arose from interest and penalties from delays in repayment. While one cannot justify the irresponsibility of past government on this issue it is difficult to expect the ordinary and suffering people of Nigeria to accept that a four-fold increase in the debt profile in a decade and a half is not the result of some diabolical conspiracy.Only any few investment in the international market place can routinely give that kind of return.With these salient but unfortunate observation made by professor Anya of the Nigeria economic summit group I passionately wish to inform you that the present social and political come economic arrangement in Africa is retrogressive and vision-less and as such quite incapable to instigate the required sustained renaissance capable of extricating African from the contemporary pitiable situation in the present global arrangement

Significant among the reasons justifying the need for change in approach and consciousness as regards development and governance is the deep rate of corruption and mismanagement that is associated with the present leaderships of states in Africa Nigeria government has calculated that $15.5 billion had been stolen and stashed away in foreign bank accounts by official of the previous administration. According to Chief Phillip Asiodu, chief economic adviser to one time Nigeria's president, Chief OlusegunObasanjo; $2.2billion of this could be traced to former military rulers. Nigeria have about $40 billion in private bank account abroad enough to pay off the country huge debt profile of about US billion dollars. This large sum went into private pockets through outright lootsof national treasury and outright diversion of proceeds from the export of rich mineral deposit like crude oil, diamond, copper, Gold, iron etc as well as cash crop like cocoa, ginger, tea, coffee, palm oil, groundnut, etc. also this large sum went into private pocket through outright looting and diversions of loans and all forms of financial facilities acquired from donor agencies and institutions. These were not channeled into the project for which they were acquired rather they go into huge jamborees, political settlement and private pocket of top government functionaries.The IMF and other major donor halted funding to Kenya in July 1997 citing the government failure to stamp out official corruption which has been millions of shelling going from the government treasury into the pocket of a few individuals close to power. Why we must ask of giving credit facilities to irresponsible conscienceless money mongers in capital cities across African continents. I am convinced that this is grand agenda to further the perpetuation of the domination and marginalization of Africa through neo colonialism which its main instrument of oppression is economic disempowerment. The dissipation and brazen stagnation of Africa is further strengthened by the disadvantage position she is placed in the global trade arena through a contemporary agent of economic marginalization of the world trade organization.

Unfortunately this grand design for the continuous perpetuation of misery in Africa is accepted, executed by vision-less, conscienceless, retrogressive Africans and executed by disgraceful leaders who through ethnic suspicion,   social instability, dictatorial regimes ,wars, conflicts, destruction, hunger, squalor, disease, ignorance-reduces all of us to the state of nature-nasty, brutish and short. The major victim; women and their lovely children being that segment of African humanity that is free from this theater of retrogression shouldtake the lead in instituting an alternative development model that will ensure peace and life in Africa. To this end, Africa women must empower themselves economically as economic power has been the instrument that have regulated the social relationship of man in modern times.

THE ECONOMIC EMPOWERMENT OF AFRICAN WOMEN IS THE LAST CHANCE FOR AFRICA IN EXTRICATING ITSELF FROM TOTAL COLLAPSE AND IMMINENT DESTRUCTION.

REASONS

1. Women are dominant force in the production of cash crops which earn countries huge revenue and Agricultural products that serve as raw materials for industries. Yet they are marginalized and alienated in the allocation of economic resources in different countries in Africa.

2. Women are dominant force in the storage, preservation and utilization of agro product in the production of household goods. Yet they are excluded in allocation of scarce economic resource through social and culturally induced marginalization and exclusion.

3. It is on record that of the nearly four hundred billion dollars debt profile suffocating and frustrating Africans, women were not involved in the acquisition and the squandering of those funds. Thus they are vindicated of the crime of this management

corruption and lack of focus that characterized the men dominated retrogressive leadership in Africa.

4. Africa today has the largest number of displace people, caused by wars and social insecurity. About half of countries in the continent are presently engaged in one form of social turmoil or the other. In all cases women are obviously vindicated as they are not in a way involved in these wars but rather they are greatly handicapped in playing a role of ensuring peace because they were politicaly excluded through bold policy of economic exclusion of women in these countries.

5. Women are major victims of the psychological and physical torture that results from war and insecurity. They bear the brunt of incessant death of children arising from disease, squalor and deprivation. Thus empowerment, then economically Africa will witness a tremendous progress in the development and meaningful existence of young children and the promotion of peace.

6. Empowering women through money "must go to those who need it project" is most vital as it will instigate productivity, family economic security, promote life expectancy, reduce infant mortality, promote good health and encourage school enrolment and child education.

7. "Money must go to those who need it project" will ensure the economic empowerment of rural African women through assisting them economically for investing in multinational co-operations and productive and service sectors. Making rural African women secured, economically.

We of the Center for General African Studies believe that African Women possess the ability to extricate the African humanity from the contemporary mess.

To the donor agencies and other institutions that pretend to have a stake in African development, they can demonstrate their goodwill through the capitalization of the bank meaningfully with capital without interest capable thus demostrating its good intention. It is then that the conscience of Africa will be restored, and then will Africa know peace, strength and vigor will be regenerated and then the renaissance shall come. I thank you immensely for your attention.

The paper by Dr. Okon heralded a wide applause. Obviously, the point raised by the lecturer went down well by the conference participants, particularly, his historically presentation of the need for the establishment of African Women Development Bank. As the applause grew uncontrollably, the conference moderator announced the next item in the programme of the day.

Dr. Helen Ndubuisi, elegantly mounted the rostrum to announce the next agenda for the day. "Distinguished participants, having listened to the wonderful presentation by Dr.

Okon on the 'Imperatives of African Women Development Bank' I earnestly wish to remind you that it is time to conduct session discussion. The huge gate leading to the central park, where the conference centre depicts beautiful view, harmonious arrangement of flowers, lawns, trees and smooth path.

The buses finally stopped in front of the conference center. Some staff of the game reserve full of smile and courtesy led the tourists to the central park. The central park harbors virtually all animals and birds of African origin and numerous animals from other parts of the world. A lavish beauty of creation. Beautiful flowers, trees, and a very diver of animals and birds. Mrs. Bonn was attentive with an oration being presented to her by her African Women Empowerment soul mate, Dr. Beatrice Ndubuisi.

Both friends relaxing on a field surrounded by beautiful flowers and lush vegetation of green trees became deeply engrossed and consumed with their poetry. They were not in a haste to join the others as the sun positioned itself westward was now beautiful and friendly.

The melodious voice of Dr. Beatrice Ndubuisi was so clear and loud, sounding to the hearing of other tourists who are now returning towards the garden in front of the conference hall from front different parts that traversed the central park. As every one of them was relaxing at the field, as entertainment were provided by the staff of the game reserve, drinks, snacks, they were listening to the poet: the poet of African Women emancipation.

Going through an unknown path
Wondering through thick forest in a dark, lonely and unfriendly night
I was amazed with what I saw:
Plans, plot, evil conspiracy, collaboration for violence, destruction, killing and looting, war, bloodshed
I listened deeply; I perceived the vibrating sound of doom, uproar and shouts of insecurity and fear
A part of the forest consumed by fire
Producing deep flame and wide smoke
There was now deep anarchy and turbulence in the forest.
I made great effort to understand the meaning of all these and I saw wild beast at bitter confrontation with each other, killing and destroying
Others putting fire in other parts of the forest that were until recently peaceful
Some ferocious and monstrous wild beast now emerge, grabbing and accumulating Baggage's, heaping them together in a portion of the forest, while cutting down, maiming and killing other beasts that eye toward their direction.

I momentarily regained consciousness.

Wondering what is the meaning of these.

I fall into another dream, wondering through unknown path again, my mind telling me that the route i am wondering through is bitter.

Annoyed and saddened by events taking place at its left and right sides.

I now turned to the right side; I saw abandoned site, uncompleted houses, and structures in ruin.

Bad roads, disused cars, machines and house-hold utilities left to rot away in the open.

On my left side was impoverished woman breast feeding her little child, empty feeding bottles, empty pots, empty plates and atmosphere of pains and insecurity.

This pathetic picture made me to be uncomfortable.

I hastened to live that scene.

As I proceeded afar from the scene of fear, terror and torment.

I came close to multitude of people.

They look like people returning from war.

Their hands were stained with blood.

They looked malnourished and faint.

They were annoyed, worn out and depressed.

Momentarily they dropped their war implements on the ground .

They held themselves hand to hand and in chain like manner, form an elaborate rhythmic circle.

And they in a frenzy swift commenced the destruction of their war implements, bringing all the crafts of destruction into tater and complete ruin and finally heaped together and set them ablaze.

They turned around, leaving the consuming inferno to bring the war materials to ruin, falling towards me, I was deeply terrified.

I wanted to run, but I couldn't move, I couldn't even lift my feet.

I wanted to shout, I couldn't, I haven't got the strength.

They approached, held me, and gently lifted me up to a tall platform and informed me that from now onwards, I am their leader.

They have collectively resolved to hand over power and all resources to my care, for proper, honest and fair distribution to forestall war and bitter scramble.

One hefty and muscular member of the warriors came to me with a very loud and persuasive voice, told me to summon other women to come and run the affairs in the forest to forestall future war and fire in the forest.

I now regained strength; I asked them, why do you prefer the women to run the affairs of the forest?

In unison, they chorused, because you are honest, peaceful and caring.

Therefore, we have resolved that you should manage on behalf of all of us all the affairs in the forest, I now asked them to permit me to go and inform other women, as I can't run the affairs of the forest alone

You can't go that way they told me; we are going to make you our king.

Hand over to you the staff of office and authority and give you a number of soldiers to guide you.

I told them that, I don't need soldiers, but I need artisans, farmers, Medicine men and women.

I told them that my ruler ship in association with other women is going to be peaceful; that there is not going to be war in the forest.

Women will guarantee members of the forest peace, fair and equal distribution of all resources in the forest.

They were now happy, the doubt in their face over as their refusal for soldiers to guide me was now removed; they surround me and placed a crown on my head.

And began to beat their drums, blew their trumpet and began to dance.

Their drumming, singing became so loud that numerous women that fled out of the forest began to return in large numbers.

The women, four in number now climbed the platform, two standing by my left and two by my right.

We in unison asked the drummers to stop drumming, which bring about a momentary silence.

We, simultaneously with the other women pledge to bring lasting peace in the forest through fair and honest management and distribution of all resources in the forest.

We collectively agreed that we would not accept war and set fire again to the forest.

Finally every one collectively endorsed peace, progress and prosperity.

Now the drumming and singing resumed once more with more responses.

In the swiftness of the dancing, the chorus of the warriors was livid.

Women will lead us, women will give us peace, and women are honest, Women will forestall war, women are peaceful, women will protect the forest, no more war, no more fire, and there is peace in the forest.

There is progress in the forest; there is prosperity in the forest.

The moderator now alerted the participants for the final session of the conference in her words, "Distinguished ladies and gentlemen, we are now going into committee sessions for intensive discussion on crucial areas, and we will make our conclusion after which our reports from the sectional deliberations would be openly considered by all of us.

Already the protocol officers have notified you of the sectional meeting schedule. The first   section is the economic section. The objective of economic section is discussions on strategies for the establishment and smooth take off of AFRICAN WOMEN DEVELOPMENT BANK. After the economic section, we shall observe a lunch break after which we shall be back for the network and advocacy session. The major objective of this session is the building of network and solidarity among African women, particularly in ensuring a fairer global order in trade and development. I earnestly thank you for your wonderful co-operation.

As series of contributions and submissions were made on the procedure for the establishment and sustainability of African women development bank, the repertoire for the session drew the appropriate summary of the session. The repertoire, Mrs. Beatrice Koloma made to the stage to submit the summary of the sectional deliberation to the conference moderator, Dr. Beatrice Uche, thus signaling the end of the session.

"Distinguish participants, I humbly wish to inform you of the formal submission of the summary of the entire reports, submissions and contribution made during this useful session from a distinguished colleague, Mrs. Beatrice Koloma, representing a known women Empowerment group in Liberia, West Africa. The entire submission relating to strategy for the smooth take off of Africa Women Development Bank: Method of capitalization, administrative mechanism and its general expectation and target are well spelt out. I hereby with due respect inform you of the economic session of this conference. The members of the protocol will now assist us to the Banquet Hall for the lunch break. I thank you immensely."

The banquet hall of the International conference center, Abuja, Nigeria was replete with cheers, exchange of pleasantries by about one thousand nationals that were drawn to the scene to have their lunch. Busy waiters and waitresses assisted by the conference protocol officers were busy moving in and out of the venue to ensure that everyone in the hall received the best of hospitality. The hall was a beautiful display of continental and national dishes which were obviously being enjoyed by the marmot crowd.

The scene provided an opportunity for further exchange of ideas and discussions on the just concluded session. In one of the tables were Dr. Helen Ndubuisi and two other nationals, one of them, Mrs. Mary Bonn a British citizens.

Helen, I am Mary Bonn, It is nice meeting you Mrs. Bonn. I hope you have had a wonderful time being in Nigeria, Retorted Helen. "Oh sure, this is a wonderful place, the hospitality, the conference, the serenity and beauty of the environment, oh all are great." Responded Mrs. Bonn full of zest.

Helen, I want to suggest that the creation of a trust fund by African governments to be managed by the bank should serve as one of the vital means of capitalization of the bank. This is imperative since the bank is pan African and more over the women have a justified claim to such a fund judging from their marginalization and exclusion for decades in the economic and political sectors of the countries", oh! This is a wonderful idea Mrs. Bonn, it was included in my submission, reminded Helen.

"I am well informed of your submission, you talked about a trust fund but failed to emphasize that the fund must be pooled together by African countries. I am convinced that such a fund must be pooled together by African countries. I am convinced that such a fund must to a reasonable extent come from contribution of countries in the continent" snapped Mrs. Bonn. Helen at this point was nodding her head in admiration.

Mrs. Bonn continued, "Apart from the Trust fund, the bank could receive fund through outright investment by western donor agencies and countries in its total capital accumulations, "Suggested Mrs. Bonn.

"I thank you immensely Mrs. Bonn, I am highly satisfied by your commitment and deep sense of mission towards the actualization of African Women Development Bank. May I inform you that I will recommend you strongly for membership of the final committee for the final takeoff of the Bank – I mean the project implementation committee.

It will be my pleasure to serve with the best of my ability in any capacity necessary." Responded Mrs. Bonn. "Thank you very much Mrs. Bonn!" It's my pleasure" responded Mrs. Bonn. Most of the participants are now making pronouncement for the continuation of other items in the agenda for the day.

The moderator, Dr. Helen Ndubuisi was once again in charge. "Distinguish discussant I thank you immensely for your wonderful contributions; incisive input, useful suggestions that have made up the final report for economic session, it has been a wonderful report out of a networking session, with due modesty I now hand over to the session chairperson, Dr. Abigail Zulu from south Africa. Thanks for your co-operation". Thus heralded the commencement of the advocacy and networking session. At the end of the entire session reports, there were further discussions and submissions on the report, which finally led to a communiqué which the entire conference participants called- The grand plan for African renaissance.

THE GRAND PLAN FOR AFRICAN RENAISSANCE THROUGH AFRICAN WOMEN DEVELOPMENT BANK-ON LINE

AFRICAN WOMEN DEVELOPMENT BANK ON-LINE: WHAT IT IS ALL ABOUT?

This is an online finance institution that poll resources from investors and donors for onward disbursement to rural women co-operatives and community in rural African.

It operates through an accurate and effective documentation of all women development institutions and organizations, rural banks, community banks, co-operative organizations, women development societies and networks, rural women trade associations, etc.

This effective documentation is conducted by our affiliate organization; the African independent monitoring group; who closely interact with these groups enlightening them through training and impacting of skill on banking information technology, business management as well as Agricultural and production skill

African Development Bank 0n line, through its research and project implication outfit, the African Independent monitoring group is on the process of documenting a comprehensive data of all rural cooperative, community bank, women development organization and network, rural women trade association, agricultural and production cooperatives, etc, with a view to channel fund to them for onward disbursement to their members. The disbursement which shall be interest free would be strictly monitored by the African Monitoring group to ensure its honest and effective utilization.

AFRICAN WOMEN DEVELOPMENT BANK ON-LINE/POINT OF DEPARTURE

This idea is born out the urgency which addressing the un-told squalor and misery of rural African women deserve. Towards achieving the objective of assisting rural African women urgently with interest free micro credit, a comprehensive on-line data of rural women cooperative societies, community banks, women based organizations for each country will be established. This data bank shall have important information such as:

1. Geographical data-country, province, community and village.
2. Membership-number of members, their names, their age, occupation – the skill of each of the member, profession and training acquired.
3. Education – the academic qualified of each person in the group.
4. Income premium – The total income earned by each member in the group per annum.

These characteristics would be represented by each of the community bank, co-operative societies or women associations/networks that would be identified by AFRICAN WOMEN DEVELOPMENT BANK ON-LINE.

The representative of each country would be serving as a veritable representative of a net work of all the relevant women development organization and institutions in each country. The entire representatives of all countries will from the nucleus of NETWORK FOR THE RIGHT OF AFRICAN WOMEN from which the board of AFRICAN WOMEN DEVELPMOMENT BANK ON LINE will emerge.

The African women development bank online board of trustees would oversee the activities of its practical research and project implementation outfit; the African independent monitoring group. The board shall be selected and endorsed by the participants.

AFRICAN WOMEN DEVELOPMENT BANK ON-LINE MODE OF OPERATION/CAPITALIZATION

The mode of operation is achieved on the principle that money must go to those who needs it. All restrictions must be removed. This is a new development model that is practical, pragmatic, result oriented and human.

African women development bank on-line should operate through a comprehensive, in-depth documentation of the activities of rural women appreciating their strives, toil, courage, need, effort and channel resources to them, give them training, skill acquisition, education and enlightenment.

Development model must not originate out of ignorance of cultural, anthropological and social peculiarities of people. Those who feel it know it, therefore this concept 'The money must go to those who need it; it should be sustained through continuous and speedy information network and response. The documentation of the needs of the rural people of diverse locations and how to channel resources to them speedily through the honest umpire, 'the African independent monitoring group'.

In summation, the activities of the African Women development Bank on-line include the following.

1. Identifying the needs of the rural women and onward disbursement of fund to assist them in their vocations.
2. The empowerment of rural women through credit facilities to acquire shares in the major economic sectors, of their respective countries – Oil, Communication, Aviation, Transport, Housing, Health sectors, etc.

3. Training of rural women in special skills and impacting information technologies to boost their communication efficiency.

CAPITALIZATION

The capitalization of African women development bank on-line must as a matter of necessity, urgently be pursued with vigor by Africans, Africans in the Diaspora, donor agencies, donor countries, co-operate establishments, multinational outfits and philanthropic institutions as well as meaningful investors from all parts of the globe.

It is imperative that money must go to those who need it! If senseless, vision-less, shameless, conscienceless, irresponsible, rascals could borrow huge amounts from banks and donor agencies and turn around to divert same to their private pocket and in return give African women war, suffering and instant death, then African women who are the conscience of Africans ever need more assistance and recognition from these countries, donor agencies, institutions and co-operate bodies.

The support and capital aid to African women development bank on-line is a support made with good conscience and it is a support that has an assurance of accomplishing its purpose.

Below is the conceptual detail of the project.

THE CONCEPT

The Africa women development Bank on-line is an Internet banking project that operates through a detailed and comprehensive documentation of all the rural women groups; co-operative society and micro-financebanks – highlighting their special features such as numerical strength, occupation, literacy level, income per annum, vocation and training for easy accessibility in disbursement of fund and other economic empowerment facilities like training and equipment to them.

Presently, the African women development Bank on-line is in the process of collecting and documenting a detailed data of all the rural co-operative societies, women groups and associations as well as community banks/rural money lenders under its present project, the MONEY MUST GO TO THOSE WHO NEED IT PROJECT aimed at poverty alleviation and empowering rural Africa women economically. The project affects the countries in the continent.

This pragmatic, radical economic and development model aimed at assisting, sustaining and developing rural agriculture and small scale industrial activities and trade of rural women will operate through giving them financial assistance that will attract little or no interest. Equally the documentation will be a valuable data bank for proper planning, development and implementation of developmental policies and initiatives aimed at eradicating poverty, squalor, misery and disease among the rural African women.

The African women development Bank on-line would equally provide other services such as the market, thereby promoting their economic base. It would equally provide other services such as advice on investment, industrial management, small holder investment and management as well as assisting them to invest in big and multinational industries.

THE ACTION

All registered community based women groups and co-operative societies; women professional bodies, market women organizations, rural women groups, religious women bodies etc, the community banks and the local thrift societies should obtain the African women development Bank on-line data format and registration form from any nearby post office across the country. It is free.

1. All the documented women organizations would receive funding for agriculture and industrial activities.
2. All the documented women organizations would have training and facilities for medium and small scale production.
3. All the documented women organizations would have their products sold at a very good and competitive price at international markets.
4. All the documented women organizations would receive financial support for investment in blue chip co-operatives.
5. All the documented women organizations would receive these funds directly without bottle necks or middle men, as they will all have identification number that will accelerate speedy attention to their needs.

THE BENEFIT

This is a new millennium development model aimed at honest and sincere private sector drive, towards economic redistribution and empowerment of rural women, for the realization of a collective goal of total eradication of poverty, misery and insecurity among rural women in African in the new millennium.

Towards this end, global funds for women, world economic forum, world women bank and planet finance are expected tolead other co-operate and global outfits in the take off of the project. Therefore, after the formal inauguration and establishment of the fund .All the documented organizations will have identification number.

A TOUR TO YANKARI GAME RESERVE

The trip to Yankari turned out to be a huge relieve to the tourists: relieving them of untold mental torture, psychological pain and deep worry which the pitiable state of Africa have inflicted. The release emerges from beautiful and bountiful aesthetic harmony lavishly bestowed on this earthly paradise tucked in the savanna region of Northern Nigeria. The obvious beauty, harmony, security of this environment depicts hope for Africa.

Looking through the window the tourists captured the reality of the deprivation of women and children in rural Africa, as the bus is moving rapidly, scores of rural women and little children were busy under the scorching sun planting grains.

A conversation ensued between Mrs. Bonn and Dr. Uche: Mrs. Bonn could you imagine the level of deprivation these rural women are subjected to working with crude implements and no assistance of any type from governments.

I hope and strongly believe that this quest for economic quest for economic independence for African women will not only improve their welfare and total empowerment but the total development and progress of the entire humanity in the continent' retorted Mrs. Bonn. Approaching the huge entrance that read, Welcome to Yankari Games Reserve, the bus after reducing its speed for brief security formality, moved through the right wing of the Yankari Games Reserve.

The ride to Yankari games reserve turned out to be smooth, interesting and memorable. About a hundred of the participants stayed to par take in the tour of some interesting sites in the country-side. Yankari is in Bauchi state, Nigeria; it is about two hundred and fifty kilometers from Abuja the conference venue.

Sitting by the side of Dr. Okon is Mrs. Bonn, a British national representing one of the non-governmental organizations based in Britain in the conference.

Dr. Okon I wonder why your country has not witnessed a tremendous success in its developmental drive, the weather is favorable, there is good land, solid minerals, large population, skilled manpower". I really appreciate your concern interrupted Dr. Okon 'But the truth is that there is yet no visibledevelopment. For instance the present government promised to reactivate all the decayed social infrastructures but unfortunately, after huge public expenses nothing worthwhile has been achieved, most parts of the country are still not electrified, we discovered that the present government since its inception on may 29, 1999 has spent huge sums as much as three billion US dollars for the reactivation of the power sector, with no results, yet it finds it imperative to invest One Hundred Billion Naira, about one billion US dollars in the construction of a stadium at Abuja the nation's capital city.

Both discussants momentarily kept quiet and spontaneously chorused the 'African need for an alternative developmental model'.

As the Marco-polo model luxury bus was moving at moderate speed. Dr. Helen Ndubuisi was busy reviewing the draft strategy for the collection of the data for the African women development bank on-line.

Having heard the information, publicity and networking committee during the final lap of the conference; the duty of spear heading the effective and detailed collection of data of women groups and community banks in the country fell on her.

INVESTING FOR A COMPLETE CHANGE

Investing for a complete change implies a humane equitable approach to redistribution of wealth. The main objective is the involvement of the poor and vulnerable rural women as major stakeholders of multinational co-operations that control the economy of the nations.

ANALYSIS

The World Bank gives African women development banks a one billion US dollar credit to be fully repaid in ten years' timewith less than two% interest. The bank in turn uses the credit to invest for one million African women on one thousand dollar per recipient. The effect of this economic approach are the following:-

1. Donor agencies like World Bank/IMF would assist rural African Women to be partakers in the present era of globalization and as such reduce economic vulnerability.

2. Making rural African Women stake holders of giant multinational co-operations that dominate the oil and gas sectors, communication sectors, financial, energy , aviation and shipping sectors in African will improve their economic security and by extension that of Africa in this era of GLOBALISATION. The present economic and social stagnation going in African will be meaningless unless the rural African Women were made stake holders in the privatized multinational and government enterprises.

STRATEGY

The cordial objective of investing for a complete change is to ensure that rural African women empowered economically through the acquisition of shares/stock in stable giant multinational industries. The World Bank and IMF have a moral duty of assisting the rural women to become share holders and investors in giant multinational co-operations.

The financial assistance/loan would be regulated and managed by African women development bank under the monitoring of the lender, the World Bank.

A QUEST FOR SELF DETERMINATION: THE APPLICATION OF INVESTING FOR A COMPLETE CHANGE CONCEPT

Being a communiqué by the organizing committee of the African women development bank project, Centre for General African Studies on the 2nd February 2010.

A quest for self determination aptly captures the nature of the urgency required in extricating the African populace from death and extinction.

A quest for self determination aptly captures the group of the vulnerable group who must strive to protect themselves or face total extermination propelled by grave social dysfunction and mismanagement, grave insecurity, disease, squalor and hunger.

A quest for self determination is the strong call and active push towards a new vale system, reorientation which applies the negation of the present irresponsible and destructive development systems that bred corruption, war and death and replacing them with sound, humane, moral and humanistic socio-economic paradigm that will ensure equity, justice, fairness, and dignity of all gender. This new and morally acceptable models is called: INVESTING FOR A COMPLETE CHANGE.We are aware of the grave danger facing our collective aspiration as a result of wars, alarming insecurityt and socks and political insanity as a result of struggle for power by greedy, irresponsible men in different countries of Africa.

We are aware of the myriads of problems, alarming rate of poverty, penury, squalor, want, hunger, disease and death that African women and their children go through, is unacceptable andpitiable in the midst of plenty; fertile arable farming lands, large deposit of minerals and well endowed man power.

We are not ignorant of the countless dubious policies and failed projects criminally executed by dubious governments and irresponsible and reckless international donor agencies in most countries of Africa particularly Nigeria which have made worse its economic circumstances by a suffocating debt profile.

We are not ignorant of the massive looting of public treasury with the pretext of providing people oriented programme like universal primary education, free health care for children and subsidized health services for pregnant and nursing women.

All these are happening at frightening sweep in the midst of dubious policies and the charade called anti-corruption crusade in most countries.

All these are happening at a time when there is so much noise about economic growth and development through prudent management and accountability.

Considering the fact that in spite of all jamborees, fiesta, carnivals called economic summits and peace and development summits nothing tangible has been achieved.We must chart the course of our fate, our destiny is in our hand.

This must be through the repulsion and rejection of the unacceptable system and replace it with a better and progressive one.

This must be through the aggressive and persuasive adoption and implementation of the equitable , just, moral, harmonious, development oriented , sustainable, progressive socio-economic development model for new Africa and a new world, The 'INVESTING FOR A COMPLETE CHANGE'.

What do we mean by INVESTING FOR A COMPLETE CHANGE? Simply put, it is an economic and developmental approach in which donor agencies use their fund wisely by investing on behalf of the vulnerable, poverty stricken rural poor in giant national co-operations through what I call the opening up option.

How does it work? This investment approach implies the proper utilization of fund by donor countries for the meaningful economic development of countries through the expansion of receiving co-operations and economic enhancement of vulnerable poor through their becoming share holders in giant multinationals.

Interestingly, the poor will no longer be vulnerable to the force of globalization being dictated by the multinational co-operation as they i.e. the rural poor become economically stable and enjoy meaningful life as their investment grow as the multinational co-operations expand.

The donor agencies also can help through GRANT FOR DEVELOPMENTS an approach by which GRANT from donor agencies would be used to further investment for rural Africa Women in multinational co-operations in Africa thus enhancing their economic status and reducing their chances of examination by globalization.

This independent social-economic revolution is now urgently necessary given the present stiffening debt growth in all fronts.I want to quote extensively from a World Bank publication World Development Report 2000/2001 page six under the sub heading: A strategy for poverty reduction.

"The approach to reducing poverty has involved over the past fifty years in response to deepening understanding of the complexity of development. In the 1950s and 1960s many viewed large investments physical capital and infrastructure as the primary means of development.

In the 1970s awareness grew that physical capital was not enough and that at least as important were health and education. World Development Report 1980 articulated this understanding and urges that improvements in health and education were important not only in their own right but also to promote growth in the income of poor people.

"The 1980s saw another shift of emphasis following the debt crisis and global recession and the contrasting experiences of East Asia and Latin America, South Asia and sub-Sahara Africa. Emphasis was placed on improving economic management and allowing greater play for market forces.

In the 1990s governance and institutions moved toward centre stage-as did the issue of vulnerability at the local and national levels. This report builds on the earlier strategies in the light of the cumulative evidence and experience of the past decade and in the light of the changed global context. It proposes a strategy for attacking poverty in three ways-: promoting opportunity, facilitating employment and enhancing security.

PROMOTING OPPORTUNITY

Poor people consistently emphasize the centrality of material opportunities. This means jobs, roads, electricity, market for their produce and the schools, water, sanitation and health services that under the pin health and skills essential for work. Overall economic growth is crucial for generating opportunities no matter. So the pattern or quality of growth, market reform can be central in expanding opportunities for poor people, but reform needs to reflect local institutional and structural conditions. And mechanisms need to be in place to create new opportunities and compensate the potential losers in transitions. In societies with high inequality, greater equity is particularly important for rapid progress in reducing poverty. This requires action by the state to support the buildup of human, land and infrastructure assets that poor people own or to which they have access.

FACILITATING EMPLOYMENT

The choice and implementation of public action that are responsive to the Access to market opportunities and to public sectors services is often strongly influenced by state and social institutions, which must be responsive and accountable to poor people. Achieving access, responsibility and accountability is intrinsically political and requires active collaboration among poor people, the middle class, and other groups in the society. Active collaboration can be greatly facilitated by changes in governance that makes the public administrating, legal institutions and public service delivery more efficient and accountable to all citizens and by strengthening the participation of poor people in political processes and local decision making. Also important is removing the social and institutional barriers that result from distinctions of gender,

ethnicity and social status. Sound and responsive institutions are not only important to benefit the poor but are also fundamental to the overall growth process.

ENHANCING SECURITY

Reducing vulnerability to economic shock, natural disasters, ill health, disability and personal violence-is an intrinsic part of enhancing well-being and encourages investment in human capital and higher risk, higher return activities. This requires effective national action to manage the risks of economy-wide shocks and effective mechanisms to reduce the risks faced by poor people, including health- and weather-related risks. It also requires building the assets of poor people, diversifying households' activities and providing a range of insurance mechanism to cope with adverse shocks-from public work to stay-in – school programmes and health insurance.

There is no hierarchy of importance. The elements are deeply contemporary. Each part of the strategy affects underlying causes of poverty addressed by the other two.

PROJECT STRATEGY

This project shall be executed through financial life line from the World Bank. It is expected that the entire grace period should not exceed fifteen years. It is expected that the first five years will ensure the investment of one hundred million rural African Women in the stock market of giant globalised industries of which African women development bank will be the receiving house. It is expected that a 10% deduction would be made from the dividend of each investment until the entire amount or value of each stock is realized. This will make it possible for the World Bank to recover their capital investment in a year's time, while the remaining five years would be used to conduct further deduction to offset the interest accrued over the period.

After the deductions and the offsetting of the loan, African women development bank will hand over to the owners their certificate of bounds in such co-operations.

Making globalization work for all projects is solidarity and advocating approach which projects negotiation, consultation, solidarity and consensus between rich and vulnerable poor in the society, as against confrontation, anarchy and insurrection. This approach ensures the amassing workable approach between all parties for an effective, lasting global peace and prosperity.

The poor, individuals and countries have a duty of deliberating and presenting their view and stand on the workable approach to a lasting global economic prosperity that will accommodate all.

EXPECTED RESULT

It is expected that a data bank called African Women Development Bank on-line shall be established having profile of all rural African Women who are below poverty line, indicating their professing skills and locality as well as other essential information. The African women development bank will now receive a financial grant on their behalves from donor agencies and use same to invest on their behalves of stable, progressive multinational co-operations and manage their stock on their behalves so as to reduce their vulnerability and economic insecurity. There would be a tremendous development in economic and social status of rural African Women. Other expected results include:

1. Multinational co-operations will have much capital warranting them to diversify, thereby creating more employment and better services in Africa.
2. Women for the first time will be major contenders in shaping the economic future of Africa through their emergence in policy position of these giant multinational co-operations.

The alleviation of poverty would be realistic in Africa thus leading to the eradication of poverty only when the government, multinational donor institutions, NGOs, co-operations and individuals work tirelessly to create wealth. And wealth could only be created through the economic empowerment of the fulcrum of African industrial and agricultural sectors-the women.

Through the application, if the money must go to those who need it project and investing for a complete change, rural women receive economic life line by becoming share holders in tiring giant co-operations as well as acquiring the skills and equipment to set up thriving small holder production units.

MAKE GLOBALISATION WORK FOR ALL

The project of making globalization work for all is the coordination of the investing for a complete change project. The contemporary wind of globalization have witnessed giant multinational co-operation gaining ground expanding tremendously in different African countries, in most cases throwing indigenous industries out of market, owing to their incomparable competitive edge. Ironically, while the multinational co-operation are making huge profit and tremendous development in all fronts; technology, management and services, lost of obtaining there finished product has dramatically increased while the poverty status of the most vulnerable group in Africa; the rural women has worsened in recent times. This present state of widened inequality in the continent has made it imperative for the committed effort in empowering the most vulnerable segment of Africa, the impoverished rural women. And the only way of doing this is by making them benefit from globalization by assisting them to be stake holders of these globalised giant co-operations by investing on them through the assistance of door agencies e.g. World Bank, If they are partakers in the globalised economy. As the multinational co-operation grow in leaps and bounds, its stake holders, the rural African women equally grow in economic prosperity. The means for the actualization of this feat is through an approach to be known as: OPENING-UP OPTION.

The opening up option is the willing relinquishing of stock held by multinational co-operations or governments in such co-operation to be taken over by other members of the society to ensure equitable distribution of wealth among all strata of the society.